EXERCISE BOOKLET

KEYS FOR WRITERS

Barbara G. Flanagan

EXERCISE BOOKLET

KEYS FOR WRITERS

Fourth Edition

Ann Raimes

HOUGHTON MIFFLIN COMPANY   BOSTON   NEW YORK

Editor in Chief: Patricia A. Coryell
Senior Sponsoring Editor: Suzanne Phelps Weir
Senior Development Editor: Martha Bustin
Manufacturing Manager: Florence Cadran
Senior Marketing Manager: Cindy Graff Cohen

Printed in the U.S.A.

ISBN: 0-618-43797-5

123456789-QF-08 07 06 05 04

CONTENTS

Preface   ix

PREFACE

The exercises in this booklet are designed to accompany *Keys for Writers: A Brief Handbook,* Fourth Edition. The numbers of the exercise sets correspond to section numbers in the handbook, and the Table of Contents shows the specific handbook section(s) covered in each set.

Instructors who have adopted *Keys for Writers* are welcome to photocopy these exercises as needed; the booklet is also available for student purchase. To make it easy for students to check their own work, we have provided Answers to Lettered Exercises at the end of this booklet. (Answers to the numbered exercises appear in the Instructor's Support Package. Printed on 8 $1/2$" × 11" sheets, those answers may be copied and handed out to students, if desired.)

Students can write their answers and make their revisions directly on the pages of this booklet; the perforated pages may then be torn out and submitted to the instructor. Students can also work independently, in class or at home, self-checking their work by consulting the answer keys.

EXERCISE BOOKLET

KEYS FOR WRITERS

PART 6
STYLE

29–1 REPETITION AND REDUNDANCY

Edit the following sentences to eliminate repetition, redundancy, and wordiness. If you need help with this exercise, see Section 29 in *Keys for Writers: A Brief Handbook.*

Example: ~~At the present time~~ I am ~~now~~ sending you a check ~~in the amount of~~ $3.50.

a. Harold was of the opinion that if he submitted his resignation the group would fall apart.

b. Each and every candidate for the scholarship must provide two letters of reference.

c. From the airplane flying in the air over the sea, we could see coral reefs in the blue-green Caribbean below.

d. The sort of motel we were hoping to find was the kind that had a decent restaurant and a laundry.

e. Parkinson's Law is a law that states that work expands to fill the time available for its completion.

1. The house is a gray color with shutters that are black.

2. I'm not sure that I have the ability to finish my paper by tomorrow morning.

3. Everyone in the bus was given the choice to choose whether to get out at the rest stop or to stay in the bus.

4. In conclusion, what I mean to say is that Shirley Jackson uses suspense in a very effective manner.

5. The United States is known as the great melting pot. It is known as the great melting pot because of the diverse backgrounds of the people who make up this country.

6. The staff of the Museum of Natural History reassembled the huge, enormous dinosaur.

7. We decided to leave the windows open in spite of the fact that the forecast called for rain.

8. In reference to myself, at this point in time, I have a very good relationship with my mother due to the fact that I have taken a good proportionate amount of time to understand her views.

9. I want to become a surgeon. The reason that I desire so much to become a surgeon is so that I can bring health and healing to those who are sick.

10. The committee members worked as a team to cooperate in drafting the aid bill.

30–1 ACTION VERBS

Edit the following sentences, eliminating weak constructions and using action verbs. If you need help with this exercise, see Section 30 in *Keys for Writers: A Brief Handbook.*

Example: I am in favor of teaching evolution in the public schools.

a. There are thirteen children who have signed up to go to the Museum of Science.

b. She wrote a letter making a complaint about the poor service at the post office.

c. We had a preference for taking an early flight.

d. There is only one more thing I have to do before I leave for Seattle.

e. It is obvious that Maurice will not make it to the major leagues this year.

1. There were five delegates representing our district at the state convention.

2. Her piano teacher had always expressed encouragement of her desire to audition for the youth symphony orchestra.

3. There was a small group of students who protested the administration's decision.

4. The former All-Star shortstop gave assistance to the softball coach on weekends.

5. The story was told by Yolanda whenever she met someone who hadn't heard it.

30–2 UNNECESSARY PASSIVE VOICE

Change any sentences that use the passive voice unnecessarily to the active voice. If a sentence uses the passive voice for a good reason or uses the active voice correctly, mark it "Correct." If you need help with this exercise, see Section 30c in *Keys for Writers: A Brief Handbook.*

Example: The crowd gave
~~Marlene was given~~ a standing ovation ~~by the crowd~~ when she finished her solo.

a. Too much homework has been assigned by my daughter's first-grade teacher.

b. The well was mysteriously poisoned, forcing the farmers to leave their land.

c. The cats were fed by our neighbor while we were out of town.

d. His father's old records had been arranged neatly on the shelf by him.

e. Cattle had been grazing in the pasture by the creek all summer.

1. Security guards have been positioned at every entrance to the palace.

2. The buzzer was pressed repeatedly by the sweating contestant, but another player answered first.

3. Magda was chosen last for every team, but she still enjoyed playing the games.

4. The dark cavern was entered by a small group of teenagers carrying flashlights.

5. Sarah's fine needlework was praised by the other members of the quilting circle.

6. The sled dogs endured harsh conditions to bring medical supplies to a snowed-in Alaskan village. One dog, for example, was injured by a bear.

7. Marco wanted to attend the pep rally, so he did not finish studying for the chemistry final. His lack of preparation was regretted by him when he took the exam.

31–1 COORDINATION, SUBORDINATION, AND TRANSITIONS

Combine each of the following groups of independent clauses into one sentence
using a coordinating or subordinating conjunction or a transitional expression. Make
sure your new sentences are punctuated correctly. If you need help with this exercise, see
Section 31c in *Keys for Writers: A Brief Handbook.*

Example: I don't remember his name. ~~His~~ but his face sticks in my mind.

a. All students should learn how to use computers. They will play an ever

larger part in our future.

b. Marco hasn't turned in a single paper this semester. He hasn't turned in a

piece of homework.

c. We could study at the park tomorrow if it doesn't rain. We could study at

the library if it does.

d. John F. Kennedy was president for less than three years. He was one of our

most admired presidents.

e. Samantha's grades were better this semester than last. She was happier.

1. January 27 was Mozart's birthday. The classical radio station played only

Mozart's music on that day.

2. They have been separated for two years. They have been meeting recently

to try to reconcile.

3. It was bad enough that I left the party early. It was even worse that you

didn't come at all.

4. Representative Sheehan strongly supported citizens' rights to privacy. She introduced a bill prohibiting companies from gathering information about customers without their express consent.

5. You're going to have to tell the story yourself. It's too complicated for me to tell.

6. Perle's boyfriend always argued with her mother. He generally agreed with Perle's father.

7. Jules knocked on the door for a few minutes. The music blared inside.

8. Death Valley is the lowest place in the United States. It is the hottest place.

9. You may not agree with me. You must conform to my rules.

10. We tried everything to get the chewing gum out of the carpet. We froze it with an ice cube, we poured nail polish remover on it, and we even applied some peanut butter.

31–2 COORDINATION, SUBORDINATION, AND TRANSITIONS

Edit the following passage, using coordination and subordination to improve readability. If you need help with this exercise, see Section 31c in *Keys for Writers: A Brief Handbook.*

Salem, Massachusetts, was a quiet town in 1692. In February of that year, several teenage girls began having odd symptoms. These symptoms included wailing, thrashing about, seeing visions, and feeling physical sensations. They said that they felt as if they were being pinched or bitten. One of the afflicted girls was the daughter of the village pastor, Rev. Samuel Parris. Other girls were daughters of village families. Some girls were servants in village households. The girls accused some village women and servants of tormenting them. They accused some men also. They even accused a child. The accused were brought before the court for examinations and trials. Many accused were convicted. They were sent to prison in neighboring towns and in Boston. By September, nineteen of the convicted were hanged. One man was slowly crushed to death. By April 1693 the witchcraft hysteria was over.

31–3 COORDINATION, SUBORDINATION, AND TRANSITIONS

Edit the following passage, using coordination and subordination to improve readability. If you need help with this exercise, see Sections 31c and 37e in *Keys for Writers: A Brief Handbook*.

Two literary works captured the hysteria of the Salem witch hunts. The works were written over a century apart. Nathaniel Hawthorne wrote the story "Young Goodman Brown" in 1835. Hawthorne's great-great-grandfather Colonel John Hathorne was one of the magistrates who had tried those accused of witchcraft. Arthur Miller wrote the play *The Crucible* in 1953. Hawthorne and Miller set their works in 1692 Salem. They used as characters some of the real people who had been afflicted and accused. Miller wrote his play at the time of another witch hunt. This witch hunt was directed against alleged Communists in the U.S. government. It was also directed at alleged Communists in the arts and entertainment worlds. No one was hanged in the 1950s. Many lives were destroyed. Many careers were ended prematurely.

33–1 APPROPRIATE LANGUAGE

Edit each of the following sentences, checking for appropriate tone; direct, unpretentious language; and exact words with the right connotation. If you need help with this exercise, see Sections 33c, d, and g in *Keys for Writers: A Brief Handbook*.

Example: We have the capability to prepare prodigious quantities of comestibles.

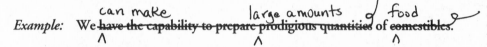

a. I went to the automobile establishment to purchase a new vehicle.

b. Optimizing their opportunities for profit maximization, the board of directors voted to offer the radio station for sale.

c. My boss shot down my idea, saying it was the pits.

d. While staying in Beverly Hills, they perambulated in the environs where movie stars reside.

e. Severe diminution of precipitation and greatly elevated temperatures are threatening the corn crop.

1. Eating fewer cookies would help me in terms of weight loss.

2. She had been admired for her pulchritude from the time she was a tiny tot.

3. Our father was pleased that everyone was on the same page about our family vacation plans.

4. Most of the money from the fundraiser went to aid the economically disadvantaged.

5. The librarian reminded us that dictionaries provide certain information and encyclopedias provide certain information.

33–2 APPROPRIATE LANGUAGE

Edit the following sentences, eliminating clichés, jargon, and slang. If you need help with this exercise, see Sections 33d and g in *Keys for Writers: A Brief Handbook.*

Example: The students ~~dissed~~ the young teacher every chance they got.
insulted

a. With tires screaming like a banshee, the police car roared off after the robbers.

b. The supervisor interfaced with each department head before the sales conference.

c. Beyond the shadow of a doubt, the novel is a masterpiece.

d. I asked my folks for the car, but my sister beat me to it.

e. Our captain tried to get us psyched for the big game.

1. Kennedy Airport was socked in, so we landed at Philadelphia, rented a car, and made a beeline back to New York.

2. The weather was extremely hot and humid from the crack of dawn until sunset.

3. My teacher hassled me when I asked for an extension of the deadline.

4. The manager had a sneaking suspicion that someone had taken money out of the register.

5. The president was bent out of shape by the constant threats to the peacekeeping forces.

33–3 APPROPRIATE LANGUAGE

Edit the following sentences to eliminate sexist and biased language. If you need help with this exercise, see Section 33f in *Keys for Writers: A Brief Handbook.*

Example: ~~Every~~ pilot must inspect the outside of the plane before ~~he gets~~ in the cockpit.

(handwritten edits: "All" above "Every", "s" added to "pilot", "they" replacing "he", deletions marked)

a.   Each foreman was warned that his workers might strike without notice.

b.   All the congressmen on the committee voted to send the bill to the full House.

c.   The new clinic helps victims of breast cancer.

d.   The Girl Scouts manned the table in front of the grocery store to sell cookies.

e.   Off-duty policemen sometimes encounter crimes in progress.

1.   Half of the international students in the ESL program are Oriental.

2.   A nurse who works the night shift must have a supportive husband and family.

3.   The firemen were becoming weary of the false alarms, but they had to answer each call as if it were real.

4.   We were awestruck by the Indian pueblos in New Mexico.

5.   I don't know if I should trust the weatherman, but I'm heading for the beach anyway.

34–1 SENTENCE TYPES

Indicate whether each of the following sentences is simple, complex, compound, or compound-complex. For complex and compound-complex sentences, identify their dependent clauses. If you need help with this exercise, see Section 34c in *Keys for Writers: A Brief Handbook*.

Example: **Many well-known actors, such as Jeff Bridges and Christian Slater, record voice-over narrations for commercials but do not appear on camera.** Simple

a. We enjoyed the rodeo at the Calgary Stampede two years ago, so we decided to see it again this year.

b. Whereas an ophthalmologist is a medical doctor who specializes in the eyes, an optometrist is not a medical doctor but is qualified to examine the eyes and write prescriptions.

c. Unless you tell us otherwise, we'll pick you up at the train station, and then the three of us will drive to the lake.

d. On October 12, 1999, the world's population reached six billion, according to the United Nations Fund for Population Activities.

e. The audience for Britney Spears's concert was composed mostly of teenage girls; the audience for Santana's concert was much more diverse.

1. If we go to the flea market, we must be ready to haggle over prices, and we must be sure to buy only the things we really need.

2. Ironically, wildlife conservation must sometimes include selective culling of endangered animals that are prospering.

3. The Ford Foundation, which has contributed money to provide wheelchairs, jobs, and rehabilitation services to Vietnamese victims of Agent Orange, was founded in 1936.

4. The seventeen-year locusts swarmed in our area last month and nearly drove us crazy with their noise.

5. The searchers looked all night for the missing hikers, but by daybreak none was found.

6. U.S. shipping ports and chemical plants may need to increase security to ensure the safety of cargo, workers, and nearby residents.

7. We nearly failed the unannounced quiz that our teacher sprang on us, but we were sure to at least read our notes every night after that.

8. The dog next door barked so loudly that we could scarcely carry on a conversation during dinner.

9. Within three blocks of campus are two Chinese restaurants, one featuring Szechuan food and the other specializing in Mandarin cuisine.

10. In the Northeast the winters are harsh and cold, but in the Southwest the winters are mild and warm.

PART 7
COMMON SENTENCE PROBLEMS

37–1 STUDENTS' FREQUENTLY ASKED QUESTIONS

Correct any errors in the following passage. If you need help with this exercise, see Section 37a in *Keys for Writers: A Brief Handbook.*

Last year, my sister Lana and me took over the job of keeping the weeds out of empty lot behind our parents' house. The lot had trees and flowers around its borders, but in the middle, there was nothing but a weed patch. Because neither of us had time to pull those weeds, we decided to try an experiment. We borrowed the goats which live on our neighbors' farm.

Goats are creatures who's appetite for everything from burlap bags to tin cans is well known. Almost anything tastes well to a goat, apparently. The goats seemed perfect for the task of clearing the lot, however we were warned that we would need to fence off any plants we did not want the goats to eat. When the animals arrived, they began chewing the vegetation immediately. They ate standing up and laying down, from morning until night. And at the end of the day, the lot contained just a few weed stalks, which helped to keep the soil from eroding.

To complete the project, Lana and I sowed grass and flower seeds in the dirt fertilized by the goats. In a few weeks, everyone whom saw the lot was amazed at the change from what had been there before. But the best part was our parents' reaction: they just can't stop talking about Lana and I and the weed-eating goats.

37–2 PARTS OF SPEECH: NOUNS

Circle the nouns in the following sentences. If you need help with this exercise, see
Section 37d in *Keys for Writers: A Brief Handbook.*

Example: Many (nursery) (rhymes) contain hidden (meanings.)

a.   In the election of a new chairperson, the commission voted twenty times.

b.   Ben Franklin adopted the name "Poor Richard" to write his almanac.

c.   Fifty chickens are cooped up in one pen.

d.   The building's owner wanted to sell, but she could find no buyers.

e.   Ticks can live for a long time under the skin.

1.   The Empire State Building was the tallest building in the world for years

     after it was built.

2.   A general encyclopedia is a collection of knowledge and information on a

     broad range of topics.

3.   The hogs were Gloucestershire Old Spots, a rare breed seldom raised by

     modern farmers.

4.   I like oranges, lemons, and tomatoes for their taste and nutrition.

5.   A new group of dancers takes the stage each time Mr. Norton rings the bell.

37–3 PARTS OF SPEECH: PRONOUNS

Circle each pronoun in the following sentences. If you need help with this exercise, see Section 37d in *Keys for Writers: A Brief Handbook.*

Example: **Each worker is expected to establish (his) or (her) own production goals.**

a. Myrna is a dancer who knows when she is performing well.

b. Everyone is welcome to come.

c. My brother and sister arrived unexpectedly. I haven't seen them in more than a year.

d. This is mine; yours is over there.

e. Even Roberto himself could not find his house.

1. Anyone can tell that I haven't had any sleep.

2. Neither of the organizations has written its agenda.

3. Pamela did not want to miss the concert, so she bought herself a ticket.

4. When will you arrive?

5. The grass, which is already turning brown, will die if it doesn't rain.

37–4   PARTS OF SPEECH: VERBS

Underline the verbs in the following sentences and label them action verb (V), linking verb (LV), auxiliary (AUX), or modal auxiliary (MOD). If you need help with this exercise, see Section 37d in *Keys for Writers: A Brief Handbook.*

Example: She <u>could</u> not <u>recall</u> her most recent visit to the doctor.
(handwritten above: mod   v)

a.   His mother always praised his neatness.

b.   Do you know what the purpose of the assignment is?

c.   Cheese is good for you, although it is high in fat.

d.   The child ran away from the hornets.

e.   I know how the money disappeared, but I am not telling a soul.

1.   The house burned down before anyone noticed.

2.   Please remind me about the appointment.

3.   When we arrived at the station, the first thing we saw was our former

   neighbor on the platform.

4.   Can you imagine a more beautiful day?

5.   He apologized to us for his late arrival.

37–5 PARTS OF SPEECH: ADJECTIVES

Complete the following sentences by adding adjectives in the blanks. Vary the types of adjectives you use. Most sentences have many possible answers. If you need help with this exercise, see Section 37d in *Keys for Writers: A Brief Handbook.*

Example: **The** _____best_____ **part of the film was the** _____believable_____

performance by the young actor.

a. They had to prepare _____ bedrooms because their

   _____ aunt and _____ grandmother were coming to

   visit.

b. My _____ dog has been very _____ since I took her

   to obedience school.

c. _____ paper was supposed to be on a _____ novel.

d. After a _____ night of partying, we were not very

   _____ at the next morning's classes.

e. They had to wade through _____ water to reach the

   _____ boat tied to the _____ dock.

1. The _____ money was stolen by a

   _____ thief wearing a _____

   bandanna.

2. Near the _____ downtown center, the

   _____ house stood as testimony to a

   _____ past.

3. I bought a _____ postcard to tell my

   _____ sister that I missed her.

4. Do you like _____ bread or _____

   bread better?

5. The crate was too _____ for Joanne to carry up the

   _____ stairs.

37–6 PARTS OF SPEECH: ADVERBS

Complete the following sentences by adding adverbs in the blanks. Most sentences have many possible answers. If you need help with this exercise, see Section 37d in *Keys for Writers: A Brief Handbook.*

Example: The ___newly___ hired operator had a lot of trouble keeping

the calls straight.

a. I had to hire someone to organize my files _____.

b. The painting was a _____ remarkable achievement.

c. The swallows return _____ to Capistrano every March.

d. He was running out of time, so he had to write _____ in his

blue book.

e. The concert attracted _____ one hundred thousand people on a

_____ chilly June night.

1. They found the river rushing _____ over its banks and had to

drive _____ _____ over the bridge.

2. Justin watched _____ as Noah asked his date to dance.

3. The old house creaked and moaned as we _____ attempted to

open the front door.

4. I thought I would _____ hear the words "The doctor will see

you _____."

5. The team closed out the series in a _____ dramatic fashion.

37–7 PARTS OF SPEECH: PREPOSITIONS

Complete the following sentences by adding an appropriate preposition in each blank. Most blanks have more than one possible answer. If you need help with this exercise, see Section 37d in *Keys for Writers: A Brief Handbook.*

Example: We drove _____across_____ the continent in five days.

a. The sailors returned home weary _____ the voyage.

b. We looked _____ the edge at the green valley below.

c. I've never known true peace _____ now.

d. _____ the long night the father sat _____ his baby's

side.

e. _____ the bridges flowed a teeming river.

1. She approached the airline pilot's test _____ fear.

2. We could see the car coming _____ the bend but could do

nothing to avoid it.

3. His parents requested an appointment _____ the principal

_____ his report card.

4. My sister acts _____ a martyr when she's asked to do housework.

5. When the temperature fell _____ zero, we decided to cancel

our hike _____ the mountain.

37–8 PARTS OF SPEECH: CONJUNCTIONS

In each of the following sentences, add an appropriate coordinating, subordinating, or correlative conjunction or conjunctive adverb and state which type of conjunction you've added. If you need help with this exercise, see Sections 37d, 38b, and 40j in *Keys for Writers: A Brief Handbook.*

Example: _____When_____Jean visited his uncle during spring break, he took

the train to Montreal.   Subordinating

a. Vera had looked forward to reading the new novel, _____ she

was disappointed that it was so boring.

b. Lukas crept quietly toward the deer and the fawn _____ he

wanted to take pictures of them.

c. She tried to sleep _____ the sound of sirens diminished.

d. We can't bring any food to camp; _____ , we will receive mail

only twice a week.

e. _____ visitors lined up outside the museum entrance, officials

tried to decide whether to open the doors early.

1. I don't have time to enter the photo contest; _____ , I haven't

taken very many good photos recently.

2. Some people say that the city should shut down the entire block,

_____ others say that that would be too inconvenient.

3. The student from Colombia missed _____ her family

_____ the warm weather.

4. Nobody can solve all the world's problems; _____ everybody can

attempt to solve a few.

5. Talented thoroughbred racehorses can enter the Kentucky Derby

_____ they are three years old.

38–1 SENTENCE FRAGMENTS

Eliminate each fragment by making it into an independent clause or by combining it with an independent clause. If a word group contains no fragments, write "correct" after it. If you need help with this exercise, see Section 38 in *Keys for Writers: A Brief Handbook.*

Example: Fritz is sick again, ~~Because~~ because his internist and allergist failed to consult with each other.

a. I'll be happy to help you. If I have the time.

b. Since 1979, because of a proposal made by the United States. The World Meteorological Organization has given hurricanes male and female names.

c. Because I have the money, I'll go to the concert. Because Juanita doesn't, she won't.

d. Captain Lowry was irritated by the poem honoring veterans of the armed forces. When she realized that the poet seemed to think that only men had served in the military.

e. In my culture, it is a constant struggle for a woman to gain the respect of a man. A culture that feels that women are not as important as men.

1. When it's noon in Boston in the summer, it's 6 A.M. in Hawaii. A difference of six hours.

2. We will try to be ready to leave. Whenever you get here in your station wagon.

3. The incumbent mayor was severely criticized by the local newspaper and citizens groups. When she refused to debate the opposing candidates.

4. The driver of the red car struck a pedestrian and her dog. Then just drove away from the scene.

5. Although Bruce never could tell left from right. He decided to become a driving instructor.

6. The result of their tinkering with the pipes under the sink, a cascade of water that drenched the basement below, showed that they had exaggerated their plumbing skills.

7. At the beach we spent most of the day sunbathing. Not swimming or jogging or playing volleyball.

8. The need to develop alternative energy sources. That's the topic for today's seminar.

9. The slaves had to toil from sunup to sundown. Never to complain or rebel or show any emotion.

10. My daughter's goals for freshman year were simple. To pass all her courses and to not gain ten pounds.

38–2 SENTENCE FRAGMENTS

Eliminate each fragment by making it into an independent clause or by combining it with an independent clause. If a word group contains no fragments, write "correct" after it. If you need help with this exercise, see Section 38 in *Keys for Writers: A Brief Handbook*.

Example: You can take the exam today if you want, ~~Or~~ *or you can* take it tomorrow.

a. My husband and I always running out of money by the end of the month.

b. Knowing that Jakob would be there. I hurried home to see my long-lost cousin.

c. The Vietnam Memorial near the Lincoln Memorial. It was dedicated on November 13, 1982.

d. My brother couldn't decide whether to name his first baby Edison or Harrison. After the inventor or the actor.

e. The lawn needs fertilizer and seed in the spring. Needs mowing and watering in the summer.

1. Tisook said that when she returned home to Korea she'd miss milkshakes. Her favorite American drink.

2. Avoid fragments.

3. He knew what he wanted to do. To win a seat in the Senate.

4. To keep your apartment cool during the day. You should close your draperies and blinds to block out the sun's heat.

5. Disposable income is income that is available for spending. After your taxes have been paid.

6. She didn't report the incident to the police. But slept with her light on for a week.

7. All afternoon, Chan searched the campus for a certain woman. The one he had seen at the dance the night before.

8. Pregnant women should not drink alcohol. Also should not handle cat litter boxes.

9. Ethiopian marathoners won seven Olympic gold medals in the twentieth century. The first in 1960 and the last in 2000.

10. Jorge hates cats. But loves dogs.

38–3 SENTENCE FRAGMENTS

Eliminate each sentence fragment in the following passage by combining it with an independent clause or by turning it into an independent clause. If you need help with this exercise, see Section 38 in *Keys for Writers: A Brief Handbook.*

An old color postcard shows a remarkable drawing. A huge white fortress-like structure rising from a mountain peak. Is it a castle or a movie star's home? According to the caption at the top of the card. It's an illustration of the future summer home of the U.S. presidents. To be located on Colorado's Mount Falcon, not far from Denver.

The man behind this ambitious plan for a summer White House was a tycoon named John Brisben Walker. Who made, and lost, several fortunes in his lifetime. While Walker was famous and rich for a time around the turn of the century. He came up with the plan for the presidential palace on Mount Falcon. He asked Colorado schoolchildren. To help finance the venture. Thousands contributed ten cents each, and Walker laid the cornerstone and the foundation for an enormous building. That was to be located just east of Walker's own home.

By 1918. Walker's plans had come to nothing. His own estate on Mount Falcon burned to the ground that year. In a mysterious fire. He had lost most of his fortune and could no longer proceed with the summer White House construction. Walker died penniless in 1931. Few remembered his grand ambitions. Except for some of the children who had given their pennies for Walker's plans. Now grown to adulthood, they still kept the old postcards. Showing the glorious building that had been proposed for Mount Falcon. And once in a while, remembered how much fun it had been to share the eccentric tycoon's wild dream.

39–1 RUN-ONS AND COMMA SPLICES

Correct any run-on sentences or comma splices. If a word group is correct, write "correct" after it. If you need help with this exercise, see Section 39 in *Keys for Writers: A Brief Handbook*.

Example: Rhode Island is the smallest state ‚but it has a lot of coastline.

a. Some people love celebrating their birthdays, some people would just as soon forget them.

b. I know someone who has maxed out four credit cards, she paid them off and cut them up.

c. My mother always said, "Don't run down the stairs," she was right.

d. When we were children, our parents let us sell lemonade in front of our house, times have changed, however.

e. He's not working now he's still at home.

1. Keeping a journal is satisfying, I prefer taping my thoughts to writing them down.

2. She rarely got to play in practices she did not expect to score a goal during the game.

3. I have never been to Italy, I'd like to go, having studied both Latin and Italian.

4. The lights went out we started to scream.

5. Some students work for their tuition, that is why they don't have money for clothes or food.

6. Although you may know your way around a car, you shouldn't try to repair major engine problems on the interstate on a Sunday in the pouring rain without tools.

7. The kettle, whistling loudly, announced that the water was boiling Andrew got up from the table and made a pot of tea.

8. Gymnastics is his favorite sport, he really loves the parallel bars.

9. Parents should be loving and caring when raising their children, then their children will grow up secure.

10. Be sure to stay on the freeway until you pass the stadium don't get off too soon.

39–2 RUN-ONS AND COMMA SPLICES

Correct any run-on sentences or comma splices. If a word group is correct, write "correct" after it. If you need help with this exercise, see Section 39 in *Keys for Writers: A Brief Handbook.*

; however,

Example: **Those flowers are very pretty, they don't have any smell.**

a. At the only supermarket in town, apples from New Zealand cost less than locally grown apples that doesn't make sense.

b. Manuel brought the cake, Patrice brought the ice cream, and I brought enough soda for an army.

c. Petra dedicated her life to Paul, in return he dedicated his life to his job.

d. Last month our middle school sponsored a "TV turnoff," its purpose was to show children that they can have fun without watching television.

e. You need to plan now otherwise your retirement income will be too little for you to live on.

1. In this chapter we discuss the skill of striking with rackets, in the next chapter we focus on striking with golf clubs.

2. For all I know, Mark is still living in Beavertown, enjoying his life, having forgotten about senior year and that stupid bet he made that caused so much trouble.

3. One problem with the free market is that it doesn't take into account pollution, pollution can be very costly.

4. Laws requiring motorcyclists to wear helmets are very controversial they don't make sense to some people.

5. Leonore drank a cup of strong coffee around 11 o'clock, it kept her awake all night.

6. Many citizens believe that political issues have nothing to do with their lives, therefore, they don't bother to vote.

7. We thought she would be angry when we gave her a list of household chores however, she was pleased to be asked to help.

8. Jack Kerouac wrote at his typewriter with long continuous rolls of paper, he didn't have to waste time sticking in a new sheet.

9. Drivers should always be aware of weather conditions for example, fog reduces visibility, and icy roads require very slow travel.

10. VCRs changed the entertainment habits of millions of Americans the devices did not cause vast numbers of movie theaters to close, as some prophets had feared.

40–1 SENTENCE SNARLS: DANGLING AND MISPLACED MODIFIERS

Edit the following sentences to eliminate dangling and misplaced modifiers. If a sentence is correct, write "correct" after it. If you need help with this exercise, see Sections 40b and c in *Keys for Writers: A Brief Handbook.*

Example: ~~Perched on the rooftop antenna, we~~ We ᵒ̸ listened to the cheery song of the
cardinal, which was perched on the rooftop antenna.

a. She asked whether the butcher shop that we patronize frequently has fresh turkey.

b. Nestled between two mountains, visitors can journey back to a town that has remained unchanged for two centuries.

c. By the day after Christmas, the children had almost broken all their toys.

d. Sensing that the students weren't prepared, the pop quiz was postponed by Mr. Sanchez.

e. Nearly having finished all the pie, we wrapped the rest in plastic wrap.

1. Strapped for cash, his rich uncle loaned Dave the money at a three percent interest rate.

2. She only saw a blur as the express train roared through the station.

3. To be renewed, the library requires that a book be brought in for restamping.

4. Wrapped, labeled, and addressed, the gifts were ready to be mailed.

5. Whenever affordable, parents in Charlton send their children to private school.

6. To thoroughly screen the job applicants meant spending hours on the phone checking references.

7. While trying to cope with the heat and humidity in New Orleans, my friend in London phoned to complain about the foggy, overcast skies there.

8. The tremendous blast even surprised the demolition crew.

9. The law firm accepted Stefan's resignation, worrying that he was making the wrong move.

10. Driving home from work in a daze, the police officer stopped me for running a red light.

40–2   SENTENCE SNARLS: DANGLING AND MISPLACED MODIFIERS

Edit the following sentences to eliminate dangling and misplaced modifiers. If a sentence is correct, write "correct" after it. If you need help with this exercise, see Sections 40b and c in *Keys for Writers: A Brief Handbook.*

Example: Greased, tuned, and full of oil, ~~you're~~ your car is ready for your trip.

a.   The archaeologists almost found an entire dinosaur skeleton.

b.   Costing more than we expected, we could afford only the legal minimum amount of automobile insurance.

c.   The job that she thought would hold her interest completely bored her.

d.   Eager to see Fort Sumter, the tour boat took us across Charleston Harbor.

e.   The picnic table and benches are on the lawn that we just finished painting.

1.   Aware that smoking is harmful to health, cigarettes are nevertheless advertised extensively in popular magazines.

2.   Although his car is old, it almost always gets him where he is going.

3.   Waiting for the elevator to come, a mouse ran through the crowd.

4.   The anthem that we sang sorrowfully reduced us to tears.

5.   Always looking for train memorabilia to collect, our scrapbooks are full of postcards showing steam engines and railway stations.

6.   To completely give up, even though we were losing badly, was not our style.

7.   Her determination even impressed the jaded movie producer.

8. Wandering through the ancient ruins, the presence of our distant ancestors

    was almost palpable.

9. He only baked two kinds of cookies: chocolate chip and oatmeal raisin.

10. Suspicious of her roommates, her desk drawer was kept locked at all times.

40–3 SENTENCE SNARLS: SHIFTS, MIXED CONSTRUCTIONS, DEFINITIONS, AND REASONS

Untangle any grammatical snarls in the following sentences. If you need help with this exercise, see Sections 40a, d, and f in *Keys for Writers: A Brief Handbook.*

Example: My mother asked me if I was going to water the lawn today or ~~did~~ *if* I ~~think~~ *thought* it was going to rain tonight.

a. Mad cow disease is where uninfected cattle eat meat that contains infectious proteins and causes normal proteins in the brain to unfold.

b. Our professor told us to pick up our blue books before we sat down. But don't start writing until she gives us final instructions.

c. The reason the heat came on is because the temperature outside dropped below fifty degrees.

d. The IRS agent demanded that Maureen bring all her receipts for the past year and could she also bring her daily calendar and her checkbook.

e. A handspring full twist is when the gymnast pushes off the floor with both hands, snaps her feet around over her head, pushes off with her feet, and does a 360-degree twist in the air before landing.

1. The history professor told June to hand in her paper by three o'clock and did she know that being a week late was going to affect her grade.

2. The sign said that cars could park in the commuter lot all day for two dollars. Put the money in the slot, take a receipt, and put the receipt on the dashboard so it's visible from the outside.

3. The reason I'm going to Honduras in July instead of the winter is because the airlines are offering an irresistible fare that expires on July 30.

4. A bunt is when the batter places the bat parallel to the ground in hopes of getting the ball to roll slowly down the baseline.

5. One reason many schools have changed their dress codes is because students weren't following them.

40–4 SENTENCE SNARLS: SUBJECT-PREDICATE MISMATCH

Untangle any grammatical snarls caused by subject/predicate mismatch in the following sentences. If you need help with this exercise, see Sections 40a and e in *Keys for Writers: A Brief Handbook.*

Example: ~~With gypsy~~ Gypsy moth caterpillars that eat oak leaves later turn into white and brown moths.

a. Our desire to climb the last thousand feet of the Mauna Kea volcano made us dizzy and lightheaded.

b. As an African American student who went to a high school in Brooklyn and had a student body seventy percent white, I sometimes could not face one more day in school.

c. In Abraham's attempt to appear polite and gracious backfired and made him appear rude and ungrateful.

d. With her weightlifting over the winter has improved Mary Jane's effectiveness as a power pitcher.

e. For all your absences this semester will drop your grade by half a point.

1. The decision that was made to tear down the theater was decided by the city council, not the mayor.

2. With my college education will help me get a better job.

3. When Samuel decided to take the first job that was offered didn't realize how boring it would be.

4. When people sometimes twist facts about themselves, such as the places they've been, helps them save face.

5. By writing this essay is to let others know that I was not always the way I am today.

40–5 SENTENCE SNARLS: ADVERB CLAUSE AS SUBJECT, OMITTED WORDS, AND RESTATED SUBJECT

Untangle any grammatical snarls in the following sentences. If you need help with this exercise, see Sections 40g, h, and i in *Keys for Writers: A Brief Handbook.*

Example: My house is as old but in better shape than my parents' house.

a.   When Noriaki seems depressed contributes to his family's concern.

b.   My aunt and uncle can and have lived for years without leaving the island.

c.   All the neighbors wondered how the two boys could possibly get away such a blatant crime.

d.   The hothouse tomatoes from the farm stand are as expensive but tastier than those from the gourmet market.

e.   The child who wandered into the aisle during the service she was quickly snatched up by her mother.

1.   With the greatest anticipation Marina looked forward her graduation from college.

2.   The car that hit the telephone pole it was demolished beyond recognition.

3.   Deirdre has always but might not continue to have the Sunday *Times* delivered.

4.   After a person suffers a long illness is when the support of family and friends matters most.

5.   One of my friends who used to work in the factory with me she told me that she could have finished college.

6. He has and will continue to feel feverish and dizzy from his severe sunburn.

7. We prided ourselves on weathering any storm until rained for seven straight days and the basement was covered with a foot of water.

8. Although very few people are attacked by sharks causes considerable panic when someone spots a shark from the shore.

9. Harold enjoys his car more than Linda.

10. My friend Jenny, for example, she applied for a new job recently.

40–6 SENTENCE SNARLS: FAULTY PARALLELISM

Edit the following sentences, making sure that all parallel ideas are expressed in grammatically parallel structures. If you need help with this exercise, see Section 40j in *Keys for Writers: A Brief Handbook.*

Example: **In many areas, archaeologists work closely with builders both to minimize the destruction of the past and ~~they want~~ to reduce delays in construction.**

a. To be comfortable at the campsite, they wanted not only to light a decent fire for cooking but also needed to have access to an electrical hookup.

b. Tom liked bowling on Saturday afternoons and to go fishing with his neighbor.

c. Listening to the crickets chirp in the country is better than to be bombarded by traffic noise in the city.

d. Bella could throw a boomerang with accuracy, clean a trout in under a minute, and could paddle a canoe expertly.

e. Betsy was overjoyed and in an excited state when she heard the news.

1. The unscrupulous merchant took advantage of her when he discovered her wallet was full and that she knew very little English.

2. In our noontime kickboxing class we find people who are present not because they want to be but they feel it's the only way they can lose weight.

3. The teacher was angry both at the students who never did their homework and their parents who never paid attention.

4. Deep in her heart, she knew he was lying but that she would never be able to confront him about it.

5. Hadi was an executive who worked long hours and never spending time with his family.

6. The umpire not only ruled that the batter was out but he also threw out the manager for protesting the call.

7. To talk about helping the homeless is not the same as working in a soup kitchen.

8. My brother in Russia said that the weather was unseasonably warm, that everything was moving at a slower pace than usual, and he would be delayed about a week in returning home.

9. We couldn't agree on whether to walk to the theater or if taking a cab would be better all around.

10. The agent told us our luggage was too heavy and that we would have to pay extra.

41–1 REGULAR AND IRREGULAR VERB FORMS, AUXILIARIES, AND MODALS

Edit the following sentences for correct use of verbs. If a sentence is correct, write "correct" after it. If you need help with this exercise, see Sections 41a–c in *Keys for Writers: A Brief Handbook.*

Example: I have never ~~ran~~ run so hard in my life.

a. We had drove fifteen miles before Mark told us about the money he had lose gambling last week.

b. Lots of people have swum across the English Channel.

c. She had went with him five times before her parents found out.

d. She sat the keys on the table with such a crash that it woke the cat.

e. I might not won the contest, but I have made a good attempt.

1. If he had went to college, he would have be a great scholar.

2. Once he got his first paycheck, he begun to work in earnest.

3. After the argument, she did left just as she said she would.

4. The mattress catched on fire because the person laying on it was smoking.

5. She was afraid to rise her hand; she didn't want to give a wrong answer.

6. Indira bought a jacket that she didn't really needed.

7. If you had took the road I told you to, you would have been there on time.

8. After lying the baby on the bed, he changed the diaper.

9. The engine in my old Honda run for 350,000 miles before it finally fell

   apart.

10. I have been froze too many times this winter while waiting for the bus.

41–2 VERB TENSES

Choose the correct verb form from parentheses in each of the following sentences. If you need help with this exercise, see Sections 41d–h in *Keys for Writers: A Brief Handbook*.

Example: **By this time tomorrow, we (will take, will have taken) our last exam for the semester.**

a. I turned down the heat, but the pie (runs, ran) over in the oven anyway.

b. It is difficult to predict what we (were doing, will be doing).

c. We were having trouble remembering that Na (was, is) the symbol for the element sodium.

d. In Terry Tempest Williams's story "In Cahoots with Coyote," Coyote (embodies, embodied) the traditional "trickster" hero.

e. Leonard (has worked, had worked) two jobs to save money for tuition, but then he became ill and (postpones, postponed) his college education.

1. I bought a ten-speed bicycle yesterday and (forget, forgot) to wear my helmet the first time I (rode, had ridden) it.

2. We had walked out before the concert (had ended, ended).

3. (Growing up, Having grown up) in a city, Leon was pleased when his boss (decides, decided) to transfer him from Milltown to Pittsburgh.

4. If I ever need free advice, I (know, knew) where to get it.

5. As the years passed, we (realized, realize) that we would never leave the farm.

6. I (am, was) just minding my own business when a police officer pulled me over.

7. The board (should listen, should have listened) to your story before they slashed the school budget.

8. When you get older, you will find that a lot of people (lie, had lied) every day.

9. If Agnes had anything to do with that insider trading scandal, I certainly (didn't know, hadn't known) about it.

10. Few people know who their great-great-grandparents (are, were).

41–3 VERB TENSES

Edit the following sentences for correct use of verb tenses and sequence of tenses. If a sentence is correct, write "correct" after it. If you need help with this exercise, see Sections 41d–h in *Keys for Writers: A Brief Handbook*.

Example: We usually combine business and pleasure when we traveled abroad.

a. They will not take a vote until all the committee members will be seated.

b. Some people looked away when they see an accident, but I like to study such things.

c. They were owning the business for twenty-five years.

d. Battles used to be fought with battering rams and siege engines, which are used to penetrate castle defenses.

e. The football coach got so upset by the call that he had stuck his head in the water bucket.

1. I believe that more banks failed in the 1980s than went bankrupt during the Depression.

2. By the time we arrived at the open house, the real estate agent found a buyer.

3. Eunice was going to go shopping at the mall, but the tornado warning was frightening her into staying home.

4. Because we arrived at the party an hour early, Renée had put us to work polishing silverware and setting the table.

5. We have tried really hard to live by the rules our parents had taught us.

6. The *Mahabarata,* written in India around 200 B.C., contained about three million words.

7. The prime minister left her residence and had driven to the country Tuesday morning.

8. According to Pythagoras, whose theorem applies to right triangles, the square of the hypotenuse was equal to the sum of the squares of the other two sides.

9. Because my parents disagreed about whether to let a baby cry herself to sleep, I have always had trouble falling asleep.

10. Recently, some communities have banned books like the Harry Potter series and dictionaries; history textbooks were also banned.

41–4 VERBS: *-ED* ENDINGS

Edit the following sentences for correct use of *-ed* verb endings. If you need help with this exercise, see Section 41g in *Keys for Writers: A Brief Handbook.*

Example: When I ~~open~~ the drawer, I saw the red sweater I'd been missing for a
               opened
               ^
year.

a.   Our office change to a new computer system last month, and most of us still

     haven't figured it out.

b.   Because she had had four years of Italian in high school, she was able to skip

     to the advance course in freshman year of college.

c.   After eight hours, he had accomplish his goal of sanding the entire face of the

     house.

d.   The school committee decided to postpone a vote on the propose renovations

     to the middle school.

e.   Once the conversation turned to adult matters, Celia excuse herself from the

     table and went to her room.

1.   Each time they skied down Tuckerman's Ravine, they risk their lives but

     savored the adventure.

2.   Nervously she smooth the wrinkles in her skirt before she stepped onstage for

     the finale.

3.   A well-trained dog makes life easier for the people who live with it.

4.   Before I signed up for an eight o'clock class, I use to sleep until noon.

5. The United States was founded by immigrants and is still being form by

   immigrants.

6. When I turn the page, I saw the ad for the new movie.

7. Molly twisted her ankle when she jump down from the jungle gym.

8. Feeling too much pressure to finish the sketches, Bonita ask for an extension

   of the deadline.

9. The parents felt oblige to attend the soccer tournament even though the

   wind-chill factor was approaching zero.

10. We were surprise to see so many people at the outdoor concert in the cold

    drizzle.

41–5   VERBS IN CONDITIONAL SENTENCES AND IN WISHES, REQUESTS, AND DEMANDS

Edit the following sentences for correct use of verbs. If a sentence is correct, write "correct" after it. If you need help with this exercise, see Section 41j in *Keys for Writers: A Brief Handbook.*

Example: He would have done better if he ~~would have~~ had studied more.

a.   When the temperature dropped below thirty-two degrees, water freezes.

b.   If the workers voted today, they will not be able to agree on a settlement with management.

c.   She would have known that the butler was innocent if she kept careful notes and paid attention to the witnesses.

d.   If he was sixty-two, he would retire without a second thought.

e.   The principal demanded that we brought a note from our parents about our absence.

1.   If the sun comes out before noon, I would head to the beach.

2.   If you had remembered that I don't like horror movies, you would not have invited me.

3.   She wishes that she went to Asia before college.

4.   I wouldn't live in a big city even if I would have the chance.

5.   If they would have sent the invitation earlier, we would have been able to rearrange our plans to attend the reunion.

6.   The residents wish that the recycling center is open on Saturdays.

7. If we began our planning last June, we would not feel so pressured as the deadline approaches.

8. If Toni gets a promotion, she would move to a better apartment.

9. It's not too late to insist that they would stay until the fog lifts.

10. Our parents proposed that we would wait until we both finished college before getting married.

41–6 VERB FORMS AND TENSES

Correct the errors in verb forms and verb tenses in the following sentences. If a sentence is correct, write "correct" after it. If you need help with this exercise, see Section 41 in *Keys for Writers: A Brief Handbook.*

Example: Someone should ~~of~~ have convinced her that beautiful women can come in

all sizes.

a.   Does a person needs to be thin and muscular to be attractive?

b.   Weight gain, trigger by changing body chemistry, is common when girls

reach puberty.

c.   Although people are increasingly aware of the damage dieting can do to

young bodies, the number of teenagers and pre-teens obsessed with

becoming thinner continues to raise.

d.   Few people are comforted to learn that middle-class white girls are no longer

the only sufferers from anorexia and bulimia; more and more boys and

teenagers of color are experiencing the same disorders.

e.   If young people would be more aware of the artifice required to produce the

seemingly perfect people in music videos and fashion magazines, teenagers

might not have such unrealistic expectations of how they should look.

1.   Although childhood obesity concerned many public health officials in the

United States, most of them agree that children who want to be thinner

should not go on a diet.

2. Researchers who have studied dieting in young girls had learned a number of surprising things about how diets can affect pre-teens and adolescents.

3. Many young girls will have dieting off and on for a third or more of their life by the time they turn fifteen.

4. A significant percentage of girls as young as eight say that they have went on a diet at least once.

5. According to recent studies that followed girls throughout adolescence, girls who tried to lose weight by dieting generally end up heavier than girls who had never dieted.

6. After considering possible explanations for weight gain in dieting girls, many researchers had concluded that dieting itself may make weight loss more difficult.

7. Some people believe that dieting actually sits a person's metabolism lower than it was before the diet, so a person's body may require fewer calories to maintain its weight after a successful diet.

8. Being overweight can indeed causing health problems and discrimination.

9. If dieting will not help people to keep excess weight off permanently, what is the alternative for those who want to be slimmer and healthier?

10. Children and teenagers should be encourage to exercise and make small dietary changes, such as choosing lowfat milk over whole milk, if they want to lose weight.

42–1 PASSIVE VOICE

Edit each of the following sentences, using the correct form of the passive voice. If the passive is correctly formed in any sentence, write "correct" after it. If you need help with this exercise, see Section 42 in *Keys for Writers: A Brief Handbook.*

Example: Fifteen trout ~~did~~ caught at the bridge over Muddy Creek one day last

    summer.

a. After the bombs had been drop, a spy plane assessed the damage.

b. The blood samples are been analyzed for their DNA content.

c. After the hurricane, donations of food and money were sent from as far away as Alaska and Hawaii.

d. The audience at the magic show has stumped when a girl in the audience was turned into a crow.

e. Two dozen witnesses were question in the case.

1. After Orlando dented the car for the fourth time, his parents told him that he was ground.

2. Hugo avoided his doctor because he did not want to be advise to quit smoking and to exercise for at least thirty minutes every day.

3. Live coverage of shuttle launches is broadcast via satellite.

4. Freud's identification of the ego, the id, and the superego as the components of personality has been disputed.

5. The single-season home-run record set by Mark McGwire in 1998 was broke by Barry Bonds in 2001.

6. A live oral vaccine for polio was develop by Albert Sabin.

7. The industrious house painter was hire to do three jobs on the same block.

8. The visiting professor was took to her office and told about department policies.

9. That theme song was wrote by the bandleader for the new late-night talk show.

10. The car has being driven twice from Memphis to Seattle.

43–1 SUBJECT-VERB AGREEMENT

Circle the verb that agrees with the subject in each of the following sentences. If you need help with this exercise, see Section 43 in *Keys for Writers: A Brief Handbook*.

Example: All of the students (go, goes) home for the weekend.

a.   Nobody (know, knows) when the new skateboard park will be built.

b.   The coach as well as the captains (lead, leads) the pep rallies.

c.   She and I (talk, talks) every day about her garden.

d.   There (is, are) five reasons for you to vote this year.

e.   Another group of candidates (has, have) dropped out of the race because of

the scandal.

1.   The district attorney along with his assistants (plan, plans) to attend the

press conference.

2.   My strong feelings about a multicultural curriculum (has, have) not changed.

3.   Because everyone in the four classes (want, wants) to attend the play, we

will have to hire two buses.

4.   Peas (is, are) his favorite vegetable.

5.   A group of us (drive, drives) to the beach every Sunday; most of us (show,

shows) up at work with a sunburn on Monday.

6.   Here (is, are) the proposals for the new middle school.

7.   My opinion of the paintings (is, are) that they are just competent, but his

(is, are) that they are exceptional.

8. On top of the bookcase (is, are) my hat and scarf.

9. Several of the students (is, are) doing volunteer service during January

   break.

10. (Do, Does) the pitcher and the catcher make up new signs every inning?

43–2 SUBJECT-VERB AGREEMENT

Edit the following sentences to make verbs agree with their subjects. If a sentence is correct, write "correct" after it. If you need help with this exercise, see Section 43 in *Keys for Writers: A Brief Handbook.*

Example: One of the orchestra members ~~were~~ responsible for introducing the

       conductor.

a.   There was an otter and three whales at Point Lobos yesterday.

b.   Her grades is the only thing that matters to her parents.

c.   The home unit of the soldiers who were lost last week are throwing them a

    party.

d.   At the start of the movie, from the depths of the seas emerge a magnificent

    whale.

e.   Does the butter and the sugar go into the bowl before the flour?

1.   Ethel and her friends Mildred and Alice was shooting baskets when the rest

    of the team arrived for practice.

2.   The sociologist's views of a company man is very harsh.

3.   The process of negotiation, coming after months of accusations and threats of

    violence, were surprisingly smooth.

4.   My mother's collection of Wedgwood vases are on display in the lighted

    cabinet.

5.   At the top of the mountain stands several tiny flags, monuments to the

    climbers who persevered.

6. My husband's headaches always start in his neck; mine starts on the bridge of my nose.

7. Were the fork and the spoon thrown in the trash accidentally?

8. Here is the choir and its director ready to begin the concert.

9. His consuming interest were old stamps and coins.

10. The birds in the beautiful old wicker birdcage sings all day and sometimes at night.

43–3 SUBJECT-VERB AGREEMENT

Edit the following sentences to make verbs agree with their subjects. If a sentence is correct, write "correct" after it. If you need help with this exercise, see Section 43 in *Keys for Writers: A Brief Handbook.*

Example: Neither your cat nor your dog is permitted out of the yard without a leash.

a.   Every river and stream is flooded after a week of rain.

b.   Recycling or bringing trash to local dumps are recommended for trash removal.

c.   Either the sculpture or the paintings is intended for the foyer.

d.   For several seconds after the curtain came down, there were neither clapping nor cheering.

e.   Several cookies in the last batch was burned.

1.   Each doctor and nurse were on the alert for signs of infection in the burn victims.

2.   The safety and comfort of the passengers were his overriding concern.

3.   Fewer special effects in a movie mean lower production costs.

4.   Neither Pat nor Sharon think anything of walking five miles after work.

5.   Her mother or her sisters usually babysits once a week so she can do errands.

43–4 SUBJECT-VERB AGREEMENT

Edit the following sentences to make verbs agree with their subjects. If a sentence is correct, write "correct" after it. If you need help with this exercise, see Section 43 in *Keys for Writers: A Brief Handbook.*

Example: **Each of the committee heads** ~~want~~ **wants the vote to be taken tonight.**

a.   A number of mountains in Colorado are over 14,000 feet tall.

b.   Either of her teachers were willing to give her credit for effort.

c.   A great deal of pain and suffering were a natural by-product of the explosion.

d.   The dance troupe weren't ready to perform, and it showed.

e.   The wrappings from a hasty lunch was left on the desk.

1.   The equipment for painting the bridges were left on the side of the road overnight.

2.   *Rivers of Steel* were printed in big bold letters on the cover of my new novel.

3.   Twenty years of commuting by subway between Brooklyn and Manhattan were more than I could take.

4.   The protesters who march every day in front of the governor's mansion seek a pardon for the woman convicted of murdering her husband.

5.   The number of stranded cars on the expressway increase with every hour that the snow continues.

44–1 PRONOUN FORMS

Edit the following sentences, making sure that all pronouns are in the proper form. If a sentence is correct, write "correct" after it. If you need help with this exercise, see Sections 44a and b in *Keys for Writers: A Brief Handbook.*

Example: Who is going to ask the question, you or ~~me?~~ *I?*

a. Is it okay for you and I to go to the play today?

b. Our lockers are clean; their's are a mess.

c. Albert thinks that no one can jump better than him.

d. For a sundae to satisfy both him and me, it must have lots of whipped cream.

e. He didn't like me singing along with the record.

1. As far as us seniors are concerned, the semester is over.

2. He wants to show the museum to the visiting ambassador and I.

3. I have wanted he to paint the house for five years.

4. My leaving the concert early was not nearly so bad as your heckling the band members.

5. Because of Walter, Agatha, Oliver, and I, we will forfeit the game.

6. I wonder if it was Dashiell or me who made the big blunder on the report.

7. I wasn't sure that the person knocking on the door was her.

8. The academy awarded trophies to the winner and the runner-up, Sophie and me.

9. Our team members felt that we played better than them except for the last

    five minutes.

10. The neighborhood has not had it's streets swept in more than a year.

44–2 PRONOUN REFERENCE

Edit the following sentences to make each pronoun refer to a clear antecedent. If you need help with this exercise, see Section 44c in *Keys for Writers: A Brief Handbook*.

Example: She put a can of soda next to the pencil and reached for ~~it~~ reflexively
the can

as she pored over her books.

a. I got a letter from the bank about a bounced check, but they didn't answer the phone when I called to explain.

b. In Tim O'Brien's work, he recounts in many different forms his experiences in Vietnam.

c. After an adventurous first lesson, José told Bruce that he would never learn to drive.

d. In the newspaper article it says that children today spend more time watching TV than their parents did.

e. I planted a bush in the garden next to the house; now I just have to remember to water it every day.

1. The novels of Nadine Gordimer and André Brink explore the consequences of apartheid in the country where they grew up: South Africa.

2. When my flight was canceled and I missed my connection, they put me up in a hotel and gave me vouchers for cabs and meals.

3. The doctor asked whether my life had been stressful lately. It was a typical cause of headaches and indigestion, she said.

4. As soon as Christina saw Angela, she told her that she had made the dean's list.

5. The cat pawed at the mouse, and then it scooted back behind the curtain.

44–3 PRONOUN AGREEMENT

Edit each of the following sentences to make sure that each pronoun agrees with its antecedent. If a sentence is correct, write "correct" after it. If you need help with this exercise, see Section 44d in *Keys for Writers: A Brief Handbook*.

Example: **Either my father or your uncle is coming on the camping trip, and**
he o̸
~~they~~ will need a sleeping bag.
ʌ

a.   All students must know his or her Social Security numbers.

b.   In their year-end report, the company gave their stockholders the bad news.

c.   Every job applicant is required to state whether they have been convicted of any crimes in the past five years.

d.   Everyone on the boys' soccer team is responsible for keeping their own uniform clean.

e.   The committee head asked either Nadja or Suzanne to use her tape recorder to tape the meeting.

1.   All a person can do is his best.

2.   The panel surprised us with their imaginative proposal.

3.   A police officer must be ready to defend himself at all times.

4.   Anyone who thinks they can get away with cheating should think again.

5.   When an architect designs a house, he must first understand the lifestyle of his clients.

6.   The crew gathered on deck to discuss their strategy for the big race.

7. My parents grew vegetables in a little corner of the yard. This was sufficient to feed our family for the whole summer.

8. No one was able to finish their exam in the allotted time.

9. Neither the students nor the teacher could find their directions to the theater.

10. Every member of our organization expressed their pleasure at the outcome of the election.

44–4 FORMS OF THE PRONOUNS *WHO* AND *WHOEVER*

Edit the following sentences, making sure that the pronouns *who, whoever, whom,* and *whomever* are used in the correct form (assume formal use). If a sentence is correct, write "correct" after it. If you need help with this exercise, see Section 44i in *Keys for Writers: A Brief Handbook.*

Example: ~~Who~~ **Whom** was the president referring to in her speech?

a.   Give this book to whomever wants it.

b.   I asked the manager whom was in charge of customer service.

c.   Who was the director of the student production of *Hamlet?*

d.   Who should we ask to play the piano, her or Lupè?

e.   She wrote an article about who the coach intended to use in the next game.

1.   The professor invited whomever wanted a home-cooked meal to come to her house for Sunday dinner.

2.   Whom should I address my letter of complaint to?

3.   Whomever would have done such a thing?

4.   Who did you appoint to run the meeting in your absence?

5.   I forgot to tell you whom would not be going on the trip.

45–1 ADJECTIVES AND ADVERBS

Edit the following sentences to correct any errors in the use of adjectives and adverbs. If a sentence is correct, write "correct" after it. If you need help with this exercise, see Section 45 in *Keys for Writers: A Brief Handbook.*

Example: If you're not ~~real~~ ^really^ sick, you'll have to take the test.

a. If you don't do good on the test, you may have to repeat the course.

b. He acted so unreasonable that we had to leave the party early.

c. She darted quick between the opposing players and then dribbled swift for the basket.

d. They couldn't scarcely contain their excitement on arriving in Rome.

e. The moon did not appear very brightly even though it was full tonight.

1. He felt pretty good until he heard the news; then he looked terribly.

2. The officer wrongly assumed that I had been parked illegally.

3. The senator felt badly about not getting enough votes to pass the aid bill for her constituents.

4. She looked very prettily, all ready for the wedding.

5. After near failing the pop quiz, the students spent considerable more time studying for the next test.

6. I never spend no money on lottery tickets.

7. My grandmother has some old-fashion ideas, but she also feels very openly to new ideas.

8. The shirt was obviously made cheap, but it looked similarly to the one with the designer label.

9. Treading careful and slow, the campers crossed the creek on the fallen log.

10. She told the child that if he would sit quiet while the choir sang, they would take a real long walk when church was over.

45–2 PLACEMENT OF ADVERBS

Edit the following sentences, making sure that adjectives and adverbs are correctly placed and punctuated. If you need help with this exercise, see Sections 45e in *Keys for Writers: A Brief Handbook.*

Example: We cooked quickly the dinner.

a. I pulled immediately the emergency brake.

b. The buttons perfectly were sewn onto the sweater.

c. The telephone rang always when he was trying to sleep.

d. The rain steadily fell throughout the day.

e. Never I will go back to that store.

1. He drank thirstily from the garden hose.

2. This tragedy must be repeated again never.

3. Cautiously, the students opened their exam books, and some smiled warily when they read the first question.

4. The realtor sold promptly the yellow brick house.

5. While he was mowing slowly the lawn, the cat curled lazily in the hammock and watched.

45–3 COMPARATIVE AND SUPERLATIVE FORMS OF ADJECTIVES AND ADVERBS

Edit the following sentences, eliminating any problems with the form or use of adjectives and adverbs. If a sentence is correct, write "correct" after it. If you need help with this exercise, see Section 45g in *Keys for Writers: A Brief Handbook*.

Example: Of the students in our class, Mildred was the ~~better~~ best speller.

a. He claimed that his expensive new shoes helped him to run more quicklier than he'd ever run before.

b. The largest of my feet is a full half inch longer than the smallest.

c. Henry's painting is good, but Carmen's is even more better.

d. No one could feel worser than I feel today.

e. My sister and I were always competitive, but we reached a silent agreement: she was more artistic but I was more smarter.

1. Elvira grew so tall that soon she was the most tallest girl on the block.

2. The sign said that we shouldn't drive slowlier than 45 mph on the interstate.

3. The candidate who spoke last was the most reasonable of all five candidates.

4. My dog is lesser dangerous than the one next door, but the one around the corner is the least dangerous of all.

5. Martin decided that if he exercised all summer and didn't eat too much junk food, he would be more stronger than any other student trying out for the football team.

6. My mother asked me to taste two versions of brownies; I couldn't really say that I liked one better than the other.

7. Don't you agree that Dr. Zimian is seriouser than Dr. Jones about the new outpatient clinic?

8. That was the most easy assignment we've ever had to do.

9. Cindy thought that the drawings were the beautifulest ones she had ever done.

10. Langston felt stronglier than Josephine about the company's human rights violations, and he organized a massive boycott of the company's products.

45–4 FAULTY OR INCOMPLETE COMPARISONS

Edit the following sentences to eliminate faulty or incomplete comparisons. If a sentence is correct, write "correct" after it. If you need help with this exercise, see Sections 40h, 44a, b, and 45h in *Keys for Writers: A Brief Handbook.*

Example: **She likes traveling better than her husband.** ^does

   a.   Joanna's pet fish has more fins than her boyfriend.

   b.   Forest walks his own dog more often than his son.

   c.   Celia wants a vacation more than her fiancé.

   d.   Julia's paper received a better grade than Sean's.

   e.   The review said the famous director's new movie was less self-indulgent.

   1.   Our waiter said today's stew had more carrots than yesterday.

   2.   The playwright wrote as many plays as Shakespeare.

   3.   Portia wants her hair cut as short as Jill.

   4.   Bob likes bowling better than flying.

   5.   Madelaine likes to color better than her sister.

46–1 RELATIVE CLAUSES AND RELATIVE PRONOUNS

Edit the following sentences to eliminate problems in the use of relative clauses (assume formal use). If a sentence is correct, write "correct" after it. If you need help with this exercise, see Sections 46a–c in *Keys for Writers: A Brief Handbook.*

Example: The person ~~who~~ whom you elect will serve as president for three years.

a.   We ordered trophies for all the players whom we feel deserve recognition.

b.   We always prefer to debate with people who expresses opinions forcefully.

c.   Runners which stretch before they run have fewer injuries than those which don't stretch.

d.   Her swollen thumb, the cause of which is a bee sting, may be tender for several days.

e.   One of the violinists who plays in the pops orchestra will be selected to join the symphony orchestra at the end of the season.

1.   Javier wrote the letter to the official whom he understood was in charge of monitoring employment abuses.

2.   The only one of the plants that have bloomed this year is the one closest to the house.

3.   The picnickers who the ants annoyed moved three times before packing up and going home.

4.   The ballplayers voted for the umpires who they felt called the fairest game.

5.   The graduating class honored the priest whose center for the homeless has become a national model.

46–2 RELATIVE CLAUSES AND RELATIVE PRONOUNS

Edit the following sentences to correct any mistakes in the wording or punctuation of relative clauses. (The prompts in brackets give necessary information about some sentence elements.) If a sentence is correct, write "correct" after it. If you need help with this exercise, see Sections 46d–i in *Keys for Writers: A Brief Handbook.*

Example: The contract, which he signed hours before his death, will guarantee a

large inheritance to his sons and daughters. [He signed more than one

contract in his lifetime.]

a.   My mother who has worked all her life will finally retire in July.

b.   The paper, which we were assigned on October 10, is due on November 10.

[We were assigned more than one paper.]

c.   The word *awesome* that I use all the time does not really mean "interesting"

or "cool."

d.   The counselor to which I referred my brother was kind enough to find time

in her schedule for him.

e.   Students, who study every day, fare better on tests than students, who cram

the night before.

1.   She spent her time entering information into the computer that was sent in

by agents all over the country.

2.   The grant, which Jillian received, will provide her with a modest stipend so

she can continue her research. [There are other grants and other applicants.]

3.   The novel, that is written in French, is more complicated than the musical

and not nearly as enjoyable.

4. The hours of the after-school program are meant to accommodate children, whose parents work.

5. The proposal called for adding three trains to the schedule that would travel express between Providence and New Haven.

6. Sara's cousin that lived with her in the summer she has decided to apply to medical school and get her own apartment. [Sara has more than one cousin.]

7. The thing what she hoped for most was a few days' rest before starting her concert tour.

8. Mauna Kea, which is the highest peak in Hawaii, is an extinct volcano.

9. The lawyer to which I directed my letter he was the only one who knew about the divorce codes.

10. The interns which most of them we hired at the beginning of the summer ended up staying on full-time in the fall.

PART 8
PUNCTUATION, MECHANICS, AND SPELLING

47–1 COMMAS: COORDINATION AND INTRODUCTORY ELEMENTS

Add commas where they are needed in the following sentences. If a sentence is correct, write "correct" after it. If you need help with this exercise, see Sections 47a–c in *Keys for Writers: A Brief Handbook.*

Example: **Because the plane was late leaving O'Hare we missed our connection.**

a. Unlike the national security adviser the senator believed that the president needed a full accounting of events.

b. She does not know who her secret admirer is but she appreciates the attention.

c. Wearing a beaded collar the poodle pranced around the ring.

d. After being mowed and trimmed the lawn looked like a velvet carpet.

e. He hated the crowds, and he resented the long drive home.

1. When you finish reading the book you should return it to the library right away.

2. Before the Pilgrims arrived at Plymouth they landed at Provincetown, on the tip of Cape Cod.

3. Donna had a cold so she did not attend the baby's first birthday party.

4. Mary did not want to hurt John's feelings yet she could not break her date.

5. Isaac's cousin mowed the lawn and his sister weeded the garden.

6. Beyond the river the fields sloped gently toward the woods.

7. Because we could read neither Spanish nor Portuguese we signed up for a literature course in Latin American writers in translation.

8. According to the study teenage boys who watched four or more hours of television per day were less physically fit than boys who watched less television.

9. To prepare for our stay in the Philippines we tried to teach ourselves Tagalog but we had to admit defeat and find a teacher to help us.

10. If battling a sweet tooth is a common problem for Americans why do most commercial baby foods contain added sugar?

47–2 COMMAS: NONRESTRICTIVE ELEMENTS AND TRANSITIONAL EXPRESSIONS

Add commas where they are needed in the following sentences. If a sentence is correct, write "correct" after it. If you need help with this exercise, see Sections 47d and e in *Keys for Writers: A Brief Handbook.*

Example: At the National Museum of American History‸which is part of the

Smithsonian Institution‸we were very moved by the exhibit "Personal

Legacy: The Healing of a Nation."

a. Alaska the forty-ninth state and Hawaii the fiftieth were both admitted to the Union in 1959.

b. We continue to assert however that dogs abandoned by their owners should first be offered to the public for adoption.

c. John Wesley Powell who led geological expeditions into Colorado and Utah had lost an arm during the Civil War.

d. Nevertheless he decided to brave the storm and drive home.

e. Athletes who avoid fitness training will be dropped from the intramural and intercollegiate teams.

1. That man in the green shirt is the one who tipped over the garbage can.

2. Janet Munro who began singing at the age of three received her first starring role just last year.

3. Arnold was not accustomed furthermore to being ignored.

4. Of course we only wanted to set the record straight.

5. Maria enjoying her brief vacation did nothing all day but sleep and read.

47–3 COMMAS: MISCELLANEOUS USES

Add commas where they are needed in the following sentences. If a sentence is correct, write "correct" after it. If you need help with this exercise, see Sections 47f–j in *Keys for Writers: A Brief Handbook*.

Example: **My schedule next year includes American government, biology, calculus, and intermediate Japanese.**

a. It was a hot smoggy and depressing day.

b. I opened the door looked around the room and finally spotted the raincoat I'd forgotten.

c. December 7 1941 was the date that President Roosevelt said would "live in infamy."

d. The moldy, dank smell in the cellar was caused by porous walls that leaked whenever it rained.

e. Joan Bergmann LL.D. opened her solo office as soon as she graduated from law school.

1. The new employee said that he lived at 2199 Davidson Drive Des Moines Iowa.

2. "If you trust me" she said "you will do as I say."

3. The large gray house was set back from the busy street.

4. I grew up in Cincinnati Ohio and my college roommate grew up not far away in Covington Kentucky.

5. The dirty mangy mutt followed the frightened six-year-old child home.

6. "Yes, you may have two more days to complete your paper" said Professor
    Herrera.

7. Why can't we spend a few days in Naples, Venice and Rome?

8. We couldn't decide whether to mow the lawn to clean the attic or to go to
    the beach.

9. How will we decide whether to pay $25,500 for the sporty red car or
    $22,000 for the sensible family sedan?

10. Yukio assembled beef chunks, whole onions green peppers, tomatoes and
    mushrooms for the barbecue.

47–4 COMMAS: MISUSES

Add commas where they are needed in the following sentences, and delete unnecessary commas. If a sentence is correct, write "correct" after it. If you need help with this exercise, see Section 47i in *Keys for Writers: A Brief Handbook.*

Example: A major deterrent to the exploration and settlement of Mars is lack of water.

a. We should not necessarily think, that he is the one to blame.

b. Eleven, very tired Brownies, and their adult leaders were happy to go home after the overnight camping trip.

c. She had three interviews in three hours, and she was very happy about her prospects.

d. Dixie, Peanuts, and Clement, were what we called the puppies.

e. There are too many tomatoes in the soup, and not enough carrots.

1. It rained on Wednesday, and snowed on Thursday.

2. Lionel tried to find his keys and even took the back seat out of his car.

3. The researcher, who designed the study, reported her conclusions in this month's journal.

4. He excused himself, and hastily left the room.

5. The old, oak tree was a stately presence in the overcrowded, neighborhood.

6. The maître d' welcomed valued customers with a polite, understated, bow, and unfamiliar customers with a curt smile.

7. The child grinned sheepishly as he refused to touch, the long-legged, spider.

8. I shoveled the snow all day but, I didn't get from one end of the driveway to the other.

9. I returned my seriously overdue book to the library, and couldn't resist checking out two more.

10. My sister uprooted many plants such as, pansies, tulips, yews, and even poison ivy.

48–1 APOSTROPHES

Add apostrophes where they are needed and delete apostrophes used incorrectly in the following sentences. (The prompts in brackets give necessary information about some sentence elements.) If a sentence is correct, write "correct" after it. If you need help with this exercise, see Section 48 in *Keys for Writers: A Brief Handbook.*

Example: Theres a place down the road where youre welcome anytime.

a. Ill sew the costumes if youll paint the sets.

b. Sarah liked to look at her brothers's record album covers from the 60's. [The albums belong to more than one brother.]

c. My sister-in-laws house is more than 150 years old; it's most interesting feature is a hidden passageway in the library.

d. When we visited Ireland, we tried to locate the Murphy's, who used to live next door to us.

e. Their house is on the sunny side of the street; our's is on the shady side.

1. Veronica has always had problems' with her nieces' daughter.

2. The childrens' clothing was soaked from the unexpected downpour.

3. After sixteen years Silas's gold was found.

4. I don't know how many As I have to get on my report card to please my parents.

5. Little Andrew insisted on pulling the gooses tail.

49–1 QUOTATION MARKS

Add quotation marks as needed in the following sentences and delete unnecessary quotation marks. Make sure that punctuation is used correctly with the quotation marks. If you need help with this exercise, see Section 49 in *Keys for Writers: A Brief Handbook.*

Example: "Why, my mother asked me, do all your friends call you 'Big Moe'?"

a. Why were we assigned Doris Lessing's story The Old Chief Mshlanga?

b. The judge asked "whether the jury had reached a verdict."

c. Our parents used to think that lyrics like I want to hold your hand were profound.

d. I think that I shall never see / a billboard lovely as a tree Ogden Nash wrote, in parody of Joyce Kilmer's poem Trees.

e. The teacher asked, Who said, Give me liberty or give me death?

1. It was George Herman Ruth's prodigious home run hitting that earned him the nickname Sultan of Swat.

2. In *The Wizard of Oz,* Dorothy says There's no place like home, but most viewers leave the movie singing Ding dong the wicked witch is dead.

3. Sonya in Chekhov's *Uncle Vanya* says, When a woman isn't beautiful, people always say, "You have lovely eyes, you have lovely hair."

4. In his Nobel Peace Prize acceptance speech, Martin Luther King Jr. said I accept this award today with an abiding faith in America and an audacious faith in the future of mankind.

5. In the poem Maul Muller, John Greenleaf Whittier wrote, "For all sad words of tongue or pen, / The saddest are these: "It might have been"."

49–2 QUOTATION MARKS

Add quotation marks as needed in the following sentences. Delete unnecessary quotation marks and, if appropriate, add italics or underlining. Make sure that punctuation is used correctly with the quotation marks. If you need help with this exercise, see Section 49 in *Keys for Writers: A Brief Handbook.*

Example: *Bollywood,* a term that means "Bombay Hollywood", is often used to

refer to India's film industry, once centered in the city of Bombay.

a. A song-and-dance sequence is considered "essential" for a mainstream

Bollywood film.

b. The 2002 film "Bhoot," which means ghost, surprised audiences by

becoming a hit in spite of its lack of songs.

c. Shailaja Neelakanten's online article about a renegade Bollywood director,

Ram Gopal Varma, was called Bollywood's Tarantino and His Band of

Outsiders.

d. *The Art of Advertising,* a chapter of *Cinema India* by Rachel Dwyer and

Divia Patel, takes an in-depth look at movie posters.

e. Popular Bollywood hits have been based on characters from Hindu

mythology and on Shakespeare's "Romeo and Juliet" and other plays.

1. Songs in Bollywood films are almost always "lip-synched" by an actor while a

professional singer records the voice.

2. The song Chaiyya Chaiyya was filmed as an exuberant dance number on top

of a moving train in the movie "Dil Se," which means *from the heart.*

3. Nasreen Munni Kabir, author of the book "Bollywood: The Indian Cinema Story," reports that the dance number on the train inspired Andrew Lloyd Weber to write a Bollywood-style musical with Indian composer A.

4. Bollywood films also influenced the creator of the film *Moulin Rouge,* which featured a cabaret performance set to Nirvana's song Smells Like Teen Spirit.

5. Director Nisha Ganatra, who based a film on "Cosmopolitan", a short story by Akhil Sharma, used Bollywood-style songs to reveal the thoughts of the main character, an Indian immigrant in New Jersey.

50–1 SEMICOLONS

Add, replace, or remove semicolons as appropriate in the following sentences. If a sentence is correct, write "correct" after it. If you need help with this exercise, see Section 50a in *Keys for Writers: A Brief Handbook.*

Example: It may rain tomorrow; however, we will go on a picnic anyway.

a. Mary has lived in many places: Newark, New Jersey, Charleston, South Carolina, Miami, Florida, and Austin, Texas.

b. It snowed very little that winter, nevertheless, sales of ski equipment soared.

c. True friends exhibit four main qualities; openness, trust, loyalty, and love.

d. The county's water shortage was severe; many restaurants in the area stopped serving water with meals unless a customer specifically requested it.

e. The president is going to veto the bill; at least he said he would.

1. Learn your students' names as soon as you can, take an interest in them as individuals.

2. My grandfather always insisted that we eat every last scrap on our plates; he had grown up in the Depression and remembered going hungry many nights.

3. Although the wind was fierce and the temperature had fallen steadily all night; the sailing party held to its plan of leaving at dawn.

4. It was feeding time at the zoo; the zookeepers fed the animals in the African exhibit first.

5. To unwind after our last exam, we spent an evening watching old romantic comedies: *Philadelphia Story,* starring Katharine Hepburn, Cary Grant, and James Stewart, *Roman Holiday,* with Audrey Hepburn and Gregory Peck, and the all-time classic *Casablanca,* with Humphrey Bogart and Ingrid Bergman.

50–2 COLONS

Add, replace, or remove colons as appropriate in the following sentences. If a sentence is correct, write "correct" after it. If you need help with this exercise, see Section 50b in *Keys for Writers: A Brief Handbook.*

Example: At the stationery store, we need: pencils pens, notepaper, folders, and

labels.

a.   His plan was obvious, break the window, cut the wires, snatch the jewels,

and sneak down the fire escape.

b.   My favorite Gospel story is that of the Samaritan woman at the well in John

4,9–30.

c.   For her driving test, Monica hoped for: a kind inspector, no yellow lights, no

oncoming traffic, and no empty parking spots for parallel parking.

d.   Brendel was ready to go to his job interview, but there was one small

problem; he couldn't find his car keys.

e.   The effects of sleep deprivation include listlessness, irritability, and an

inability to concentrate.

1.   That airline serves many Asian cities, including: Tokyo, Beijing, Hong Kong,

and Seoul.

2.   Management made one big concession; the company would continue to pay

all employees' health insurance premiums.

3.   To restore profits, the consultant recommended three actions: cut employee

wages, increase advertising, and eliminate stock options.

4. Two anticipated effects of the storm were: increased erosion of the shoreline

    and a flash flood in the center of town.

5. The movie had a disappointing ending; the hero joined the villains.

51–1 PERIODS, QUESTION MARKS, AND EXCLAMATION POINTS

Add or delete periods, question marks, and exclamation points as appropriate in the following sentences. If a sentence is correct, write "correct" after it. If you need help with this exercise, see Sections 51a and b in *Keys for Writers: A Brief Handbook.*

Example: I wonder when spring will come

a.   Would you please give me a call as soon as you're ready

b.   "Are you crazy" he asked

c.   "The tornado is heading straight for us" he screamed. "Run for your life"

d.   My younger sister spent a week at a space camp run by N.A.S.A.

e.   With parents like that, is it any wonder that he's always late

1.   I keep pondering what's beyond the end of the universe

2.   Will you be staying with us this evening

3.   I asked Antonio if he really wanted me to withdraw his name from consideration

4.   We were all proud of Uncle Jerry, who at the age of thirty-seven had finally earned his B.A.

5.   Why didn't I think of that

51–2 DASHES, PARENTHESES, BRACKETS, SLASHES, AND ELLIPSIS DOTS

In the following sentences, punctuate the italicized words (and the spaces around and between them) appropriately, using dashes, parentheses, brackets, slashes, or ellipsis dots. (The prompts in brackets give necessary information about some sentences.) If you need help with this exercise, see Sections 51c–g in *Keys for Writers: A Brief Handbook*.

Example: The heroes of my parents' youth — *John F. Kennedy, for example* — seem

somehow more heroic than the heroes of my generation.

a.   Shirley St. Hill Chisholm *who was the country's first African American Congresswoman* used the campaign slogan "Unbought and Unbossed."

b.   The judge said, "You *the defendant* are a menace to society."

c.   His final shot *what a blast!* sank through the basket just as the buzzer sounded.

d.   The monetary part of the reward *$50* wasn't nearly as important as the recognition.

e.   In her last speech to Torvald, Nora declares her independence: "I'm freeing you from being *responsible There* has to be absolute freedom for us both" *64*. [The original direct quotation, from page 64 of Ibsen's *A Doll's House*, is as follows: "I'm freeing you from being responsible. Don't feel yourself bound, any more than I will. There has to be absolute freedom for us both."]

1. Sherwood went to his first FFA *Future Farmers of America* meetings when he was only ten.

2. Walt Whitman mourns the death of Abraham Lincoln in the poem beginning with these famous lines: "O Captain! my Captain! our fearful trip is *done, The* ship has weather'd every rack, the prize we sought is won." [The lines from the poem read:

    O Captain! my Captain! our fearful trip is done,

    The ship has weather'd every rack, the prize we sought is won.]

3. While in the Boston area, we visited four historical *places North* Bridge, Lexington Green, Paul Revere's House, and Old North *Church related* to the start of the Revolution.

4. June 18 is the birthday of two highly creative people*: me b. 1950 and Paul McCartney b. 1942.*

5. If there's any advantage to having to eat in the dormitory, it's that I don't have to eat food I don't *like liver,* broccoli, tuna casserole.

52–1 UNDERLINING (ITALICS)

Underline words and terms as necessary in the following sentences. Change any underlining that is not correct. (You may have to add quotation marks in some sentences.) If you need help with this exercise, see Section 52 in *Keys for Writers: A Brief Handbook.*

Example: The <u>New York Times</u> is among America's most respected news sources, but I also rely on my local <u>Riverton Gazette</u>.

a. The French use the term bon appetit at the beginning of a meal; many Americans now say simply, "Enjoy."

b. The poem <u>Video Cuisine</u> appears in Maxine Kumin's collection <u>The Long Approach</u>.

c. My two-year-old uses the word dog to refer to any animal.

d. Most Americans know the Latin word for tree, which is arbor.

e. I've seen the movie Master and Commander four times, and I intend to see it at least four more.

1. Do you take the creation story in <u>Genesis</u> literally?

2. That sunset was the most <u>amazing</u> sight I have ever seen.

3. The film Emma is based on Jane Austen's novel Emma.

4. The tragic end of the space shuttle Columbia decreased public confidence in the shuttle program.

5. The word hellion <u>certainly</u> applies to my adolescent niece.

53–1 CAPITALIZATION

Edit the following sentences for correct use of capital letters. If a sentence is correct, write "correct" after it. If you need help with this exercise, see Section 53 in *Keys for Writers: A Brief Handbook.*

Example: In ~~High School~~, I was editor of the newspaper *The Cardinal.*

(handwritten above: high school)

a. The mayor of New Market, Johanna Hindeman, attended the Memorial Day fireworks every year.

b. The republican party was known as the antislavery party at the time of the civil war.

c. During Fall Semester our Architecture class visited Rockefeller center, the Empire State building, and St. Patrick's cathedral.

d. Mahatma Gandhi applied the principles of Civil Disobedience to his struggle for Indian independence.

e. Virginia Cusack, Executive Vice President, was known to most of the workers as Ginny.

1. F. Scott Fitzgerald's short story "The diamond as big as the Ritz" contains a theme that would reappear in *The great Gatsby.*

2. Whether you head east to east Orange, south to south Carolina, or north to north Dakota, you're sure to find a McDonald's.

3. When did Mae West say, "too much of a good thing can be wonderful"?

4. We made a left onto Chestnut street instead of a right and ended up on Ramada boulevard.

5. The norman conquest of England, led by William the conqueror, started in 1066.

54–1 ABBREVIATIONS

Edit the following sentences for correct use of abbreviations. If a sentence is correct, write "correct" after it. If you need help with this exercise, see Section 54 in *Keys for Writers: A Brief Handbook.*

Example: Try to get that ~~info.~~ to me by ~~Tues. a.m.~~
information (inserted above "info.")
Tuesday morning. (inserted above "Tues. a.m.")

a. Doctor Roya Mullen was my pediatrician, and now she is my children's.

b. The students wondered how they would get through all of chap. 5 in one night.

c. My older brother still does not know how to program his VCR.

d. The men voted to stay overnight in NYC, but the women voted to continue on to Phila.

e. The F.B.I., the C.I.A., and the I.R.S. don't have the best reputations with the Amer. public.

1. We measured the plot in meters, not in yds.

2. Jordan Reynolds has two M.A.'s and one Ph.D.

3. My brother-in-law said he was bringing everyone he could think of—his mother, father, sisters, brothers, aunts, etc.—to my family's reunion.

4. My superstitious sister's birthday, Oct. 13, will fall on a Fri. this year.

5. Semipamis, who may have built the Hanging Gardens of Babylon, ruled Assyria from 811 to 809 BCE.

55–1 NUMBERS

Edit the following sentences for correct use of numbers (assume the conventions of the humanities). If a sentence is correct, write "correct" after it. If you need help with this exercise, see Section 55 in *Keys for Writers: A Brief Handbook.*

> *Example:*   Of the eleven people at the party,~~7~~ *Seven* were old friends, ~~2~~ *two* were
> colleagues, and ~~2~~ *two* were relatives.

a.   On December seven, 1941, Japanese planes attacked Pearl Harbor.

b.   We counted twenty-seven sailboats on the lake yesterday afternoon.

c.   To get ready for the race, Yvonne ran 3 miles one day, 5 miles the next, and 8 miles the next.

d.   Nell took exactly nine dollars and twenty-five cents from her piggy bank when she went to the arcade.

e.   12 times this year I've asked my neighbors to keep their dog tied up during the day when they're at work.

1.   Ms. Brimley has lived at twenty-five Grand Boulevard all her life.

2.   After three periods the hockey playoff game was tied seven to seven and the teams were headed into overtime.

3.   We drove 1/2 mile beyond the end of the paved road before deciding that we were lost and should turn around.

4.   The average grade on the calculus test was sixty-two before the professor applied the curve.

5.   I took 3 semesters of Spanish, and I think I need 3 more before I will feel comfortable traveling on my own in South America.

56–1 HYPHENATION

Add or delete hyphens as necessary in the following sentences. If a sentence is correct, write "correct" after it. If you need help with this exercise, see Section 56 in *Keys for Writers: A Brief Handbook.*

Example: He did a first͟‌rate job on that budget movie.
                        ∧

a. After the accident, Jake was semi-conscious, and it took him forty five

   minutes to remember his own name.

b. Three quarters of the way through the test, I realized I didn't remember

   enough about post Reconstruction America to answer the last essay question.

c. The short term profit was a relief to the fledgling CEO.

d. Her way out ideas have led to some really-innovative advances in medical

   treatment.

e. The half price items at the hardware store included a gas powered leaf

   blower.

1. It was a store for do it yourself homeowners. Walter, the fix it man, loved it.

2. The lost hiker was well bundled against the elements, but he was half

   starved and frightened.

3. In a public spirited gesture, the owners of the automobile dealership gave

   the homeless shelter the use of a van every night.

4. Because the all important high ratings failed to materialize, the network

   decided to cancel the usually-entertaining sitcom.

5. More and more anti-wrinkle creams are being sold over the counter.

58–1   SPELLING

Correct any spelling errors in the following sentences. If a sentence is correct, write "correct" after it. If you need help with this exercise, see Section 58 in *Keys for Writers: A Brief Handbook.*

Example: She was an old acquaint~~e~~nce, but I'm not sure I would describe her as
a fr~~ei~~nd.

a.   Gertrude was very embarassed when her pocketbook spilled open on the

subway train.

b.   Most young people want independance from their parents, but many of

them also want thier parents to continue to support them, if only

emotionaly.

c.   In the beginning, my writing contained a lot of awkward phrases.

d.   My sociology professor is very knowledgable, but sometimes her knowledge

interfers with common sense.

e.   Our seventh-grade teacher always told us that our grammer was good but

that we mispelled too much.

1.   Sometimes it takes the band members half a day to set up their equiptment.

2.   Do you know whether he is celebrating his thirty-eigth or fourtieth

birthday?

3.   The young violinist who just won a position with the orchestra now has to

decide whether to persue her college education first.

4. As soon as Louis gets his licence, he will be able to drive us anywhere we want to go in his father's convertable.

5. She publicly announced her candidacy for attorney general.

58–2 SPELLING

On the line next to each of the following words, write the correct spelling if the word is spelled incorrectly. If the word is correct, write "correct" after it. If you need help with this exercise, see Section 58 in *Keys for Writers: A Brief Handbook.*

Example: churchs (plural) _churches_____

a. leafs (plural) _____

b. percieve _____

c. offerred _____

d. economies (plural) _____

e. prettyest _____

1. criteria (plural) _____   6. tieing _____

2. writting _____   7. monkies (plural)

    _____

3. radioes (plural) _____   8. seize _____

4. judgment _____   9. tooths (plural) _____

5. parodys (plural) _____   10. accidently _____

PART 9
FOR MULTILINGUAL/ESL WRITERS

60–1 CATEGORIES OF NOUNS AND NOUN PLURALS

Identify the nouns in the following sentences as either proper nouns (P), countable common nouns (CC), or uncountable common nouns (UC), and correct any incorrect verbs or adjectives. If you need help with this exercise, see Sections 60a and b in *Keys for Writers: A Brief Handbook.*

Example: Thousands of tourists visits the Sphinx each year.

a. The Volga River is the longest river in Europe.

b. Many people believes they have been abducted by aliens from space.

c. Times Square has experienced a renaissance in recent years.

d. The *New York Times* employs many excellents reporters.

e. Jell-O is a brand of gelatin frequently used in making low-fats desserts.

1. All three brothers works for the Army Corps of Engineers.

2. Sue buys raw diamonds from South Africa and makes rings, earrings, and other jewelry.

3. The accountant asked his clients for more information about their delinquents accounts.

4. Fadwa's favorites pastimes includes sports, music, and cooking.

5. Leo visited the Eiffel Tower in June with his goods friends Pierre and Marie.

60–2 NOUNS AND ARTICLES

Edit the following sentences, adding or changing articles as needed and deleting any articles that are not needed. If you need help with this exercise, see Section 60 in *Keys for Writers: A Brief Handbook.*

Example: On my first, one-day visit to ~~the~~ Washington, D.C., I wasn't sure

   which sights to see first.

a.   The line of tourists at a White House was already quite long, winding along

   a street next to the White House lawn toward a park called the Ellipse.

b.   I walked around an Ellipse and up small hill to a Washington Monument.

c.   A line there was not as long, so I waited underneath the circle of fifty flags, a

   one for every state in the United States.

d.   From an information in my guidebook, I learned that the monument is 555

   feet tall and was a tallest structure in world when it was built in 1886.

e.   From observation area at a top of a monument I could see all of Washington

   spread out before me.

1.   Across the Mall I could see a Capitol Building and the other museums lining

   the Mall.

2.   Toward a west I could see the monument to the President Lincoln, toward

   an east the monument to President Jefferson.

3.   Beyond those two monuments was a meandering Potomac River.

4. Not until I came down from the top of the monument and began walking

    across Mall did I realize that a scale of all buildings masks distances between

    them.

5. I also realized that I would be doing great deal of a walking in a city before

    a day had ended.

60–3 NOUNS AND ARTICLES

Edit the following sentences for correct use of articles. You may need to add and delete articles, change the form of some nouns, and add other words. If a sentence is correct, write "correct" after it. If you need help with this exercise, see Section 60 in *Keys for Writers: A Brief Handbook.*

Example: We drove to ~~a~~ the Delaware Water Gap to look at ~~a~~ the scenery.

a. I put a potato in the oven and then went out to the store. Hour later I had to phone my sister and ask her to take a potato out of the oven.

b. The money can't buy a happiness, but it can pay a grocery bill.

c. Which country in the South America is your roommate from?

d. Jorge asked his mother for an advice about living away from a home for a first time.

e. She ordered a hamburger and fries. Fries were delivered first; by the time a hamburger arrived at her table, she had finished eating all the fries.

1. We went for a walk under stars. After the hour, it got very cold and a walk became a run.

2. When my parents set up a bakery in small storefront, they had to buy several equipments such as the oven and the huge freezer.

3. Mario was a tallest boy in a sixth-grade class.

4. A neighbor who works the night shift asked me to feed his cat before I go to bed.

5. I poured a cereal into a bowl on the counter and then added a milk.

6. The Fondinis visit their family in Italy in the June and July every year.

7. Willie turned off his alarm clock and turned on a TV across from his bed to find out what a weather was going to be today.

8. The honesty is a best policy.

9. We had been planning a picnic for the months. When the day of a picnic finally arrived, we remembered a bottle of wine we'd bought for the occasion but forgot a corkscrew to open a bottle.

10. In our culture class, we're reading a French, Spanish, and African literature.

61–1   THE *BE* AUXILIARY

Edit the following sentences for correct use of the *be* auxiliary and the correct form of the following verb. If a sentence is correct, write "correct" after it. If you need help with this exercise, see Section 61a in *Keys for Writers: A Brief Handbook.*

Example: She has ~~dance~~ since the party began.

(handwritten: been dancing)

a.   They eating now.

b.   The pool be drained last month.

c.   The skyscraper build in only three months.

d.   She was still looking for her glasses when the movie began.

e.   Ivan taking an art class for six weeks.

1.   The plane take off when the rain began.

2.   Marcia singing in tonight's concert.

3.   The cook was toss the salad when the rolls burned.

4.   The company was losing money on its new product line.

5.   That sweater made in Peru.

61–2 MODAL AUXILIARY VERBS

In each of the following sentences, use the correct form of the verb in brackets, preceded by an appropriate modal auxiliary verb or verbs. Use the meaning suggested in brackets as a guide. If you need help with this exercise, see Section 61b in *Keys for Writers: A Brief Handbook*.

Example: He _will clean_____ his room tomorrow. [*clean;* intention]

a. If the baby does not sleep too much during the day, she _____

   well tonight. [*sleep;* expectation]

b. My mother is standing on my front doorstep. I _____ the door

   when I went out. [*lock;* logical assumption]

c. If we had known you were coming, we _____ set an extra place

   at the table. [*set;* speculation]

d. I _____ the floor before my company arrives. [*wash;* necessity]

e. I _____ not _____ a visa because I applied too late.

   [*get;* ability]

1. She said we _____ away during spring break. [*go;* possibility]

2. He _____ calculus before he entered high school. [*understand;*

   ability]

3. When we went to the beach every summer, we _____ huge

   sand castles every day. [*build;* repeated action]

4. She's not on this plane; she _____ on the next one. [*be;*

   possibility or logical assumption]

5. We _____ fertilizing the lawn before it rains. [*finish;* necessity]

6. If you want to finish college in three years, you _____ your

    course schedule more carefully. [*plan;* advisability]

7. We _____ to the movies if we aren't too tired. [*go;* intention]

8. If I had written to you sooner, you _____ my plans. [*know;*

    speculation]

9. We told them our plans; they _____ we wouldn't be here until

    this afternoon. [*know;* expectation]

10. We _____ our plane tickets by now. [*receive;* expectation]

61–3 VERBS FOLLOWED BY AN INFINITIVE OR *-ING* VERBAL

Edit the following sentences, using the correct verbal forms. If a sentence is correct, write "correct" after it. If you need help with this exercise, see Sections 61c–e in *Keys for Writers: A Brief Handbook.*

Example: Claudia did not expect ~~failing~~ her exam because she had studied hard.
_{to fail}

a.   The pilot ordered the passengers turning off their cell phones for the rest of the flight.

b.   The committee discussed adopting the proposal but postponed to vote on it until the next meeting.

c.   On her first trip to Hawaii, she could not imagine to be in a more beautiful place on Earth.

d.   Tony persuaded his mother allowing him to take the family car overnight.

e.   We can no longer pretend being uninvolved.

1.   The counselor told me to try to remember as much as possible about my childhood.

2.   The bossy older sister enjoyed to make her timid younger sister clear the table after every meal.

3.   My parents always encouraged me to be independent and honest.

4.   Jackson disliked to take the baby to the doctor.

5.   Brigette finished to study after her friends left.

6.   Don't delay to send in your money for the tickets.

7. All her adult life my grandmother has avoided to eat raisins because she was forced to eat them during the Depression.

8. I will not deny to run the red light, but I hope no one asks.

9. Did the clerk suggest to give you a rain check for the chair that was on sale?

10. The sign warned visitors swimming at their own risk.

61–4   VERBALS USED AS ADJECTIVES

Edit the following sentences, using the correct form of verbals used as adjectives. If a sentence is correct, write "correct" after it. If you need help with this exercise, see Section 61f in *Keys for Writers: A Brief Handbook.*

Example: The ~~excited~~ ^{exciting} finish to the ballgame made us all go home feeling ~~exhilarating.~~ ^{exhilarated.}

a.   I am always annoying by my little brother's early morning noise when I am
     trying to sleep late.

b.   The statistics on underage drinking and driving are very depressed.

c.   Sarah reluctantly brought her disappointed first-semester report card home
     to her parents.

d.   The worried director made her exhausting cast run through the play one
     more time.

e.   We couldn't imagine a more bored lecture, but we kept ourselves amusing
     by passing notes across the back row.

1.   One of my most embarrassed moments was setting off the bakery's alarm one
     morning before it was open.

2.   The surprising look on their faces told us that our little secret had worked.

3.   Geraiut's grandfather spun a fascinated tale of life in the coal mines.

4.   Tonight's algebra homework consists of the most confused problems I've ever
     seen.

5.   The stunning family received the shocked news without comment.

62–1 SENTENCE STRUCTURE

Edit the following sentences, making sure that sentence elements are complete and in the correct order. If a sentence is correct, write "correct" after it. If you need help with this exercise, see Sections 62a–c in *Keys for Writers: A Brief Handbook.*

Example: Steve bought for his little brother a hot dog at the baseball game.

a.   The committee sent to the alleged witness a subpoena.

b.   Professor Moran explained the class exponential functions.

c.   I have to find my mother a gift for her birthday.

d.   The meteorology students visited yesterday Mount Washington.

e.   Bob ran every morning because helped him keep in shape.

1.   The library's director opened us the room containing the rare books.

2.   Her roommate offered her the rugs they had bought at the beginning of the year.

3.   Jesse Owens broke in his lifetime seven world records for track and field events.

4.   He sold the old snowboard his best friend.

5.   Are two reasons why he to the store returned the shoes.

62–2 DIRECT AND INDIRECT QUOTATIONS AND QUESTIONS

Rewrite each of the following direct quotations or questions as an indirect quotation or question, making appropriate changes in subjects and verb forms. If you need help with this exercise, see Section 62d in *Keys for Writers: A Brief Handbook.*

Example: Professor Alfonso told her students, ~~"Do your~~ to do their homework in blue books tonight.~~"~~

a.   During the inquiry, he kept repeating, "I didn't see a thing."

b.   "Plant these impatiens in a shady corner of the flowerbed," the woman at the garden shop told us.

c.   She asked, "Do you want to taste the brownies?" I said, "Sure, I want to taste them."

d.   My cousin asked, "Do you remember the summer we spent on Granddad's farm?"

e.   As she stepped out of the car at the airport terminal, Carla told her father, "Please don't bother, I can handle my bags myself."

1.   "Why did you sit in traffic instead of taking the back roads?" we asked when they arrived two hours late.

2.   "Are we going to the zoo or the aquarium first?" the little girl asked her father.

3.   "I've never been able to do twenty pushups at a time," she said.

4.   "Don't come unprepared to the exam," the teacher said.

5.   He asked, "Where are they going?"

62–3 ORDER OF ADJECTIVES

Edit the following sentences, making sure that adjectives are correctly placed and punctuated. If a sentence is correct, write "correct" after it. If you need help with this exercise, see Section 62g in *Keys for Writers: A Brief Handbook*.

Example: When we pulled into the lot we saw many red expensive cars, but we

were looking for a white inexpensive car.

a.   She became an American genuine celebrity.

b.   He plans the annual giant Greek Orthodox Easter picnic in the park.

c.   To cheer me up on this dreary day, I brought along my new flowered huge

umbrella.

d.   A yellow small shed stands at the end of her wooden new walkway in the

garden.

e.   The panting yapping dog dashed madly around our ankles, hoping for a

walk.

1.   She lost her balance during her swim aerobics class and got a purple

enormous bruise on her shoulder.

2.   That was the funniest French movie I have ever seen.

3.   I'm looking forward to living in England, but I'm not looking forward to

many cold damp days.

4.   We are finally planning to replace the porcelain old avocado-colored sink in

the kitchen.

5. The baby's room was painted a pleasant green color that reminded us of

    spring new leaves.

63–1 IDIOMATIC STRUCTURES

Edit the following sentences, adding, deleting, or changing prepositions as necessary for correct use with adjectives and verbs. If a sentence is correct, write "correct" after it. If you need help with this exercise, see Sections 63a–c in *Keys for Writers: A Brief Handbook.*

> of
Example: Are you aware the rules for claiming the prize?
> ∧

a.   In May, the dissatisfied passenger wrote a letter complaining for the lack of food on the four-hour train trip.

b.   She has always been interested of features at the moon.

c.   When we arrived at Florence, we weren't sure whether to go to the Duomo or the Uffizi first.

d.   He was content by his low-paying entry-level job because it left him time for his real passion: scuba diving.

e.   She was very anxious of losing the ticket until her uncle found it lying at the couch.

1.   After their luggage was stolen, they had to rely to the sun to wake them up in the morning.

2.   I have never been fond to tulips: they are too tall and spindly.

3.   The troop leader worried for her girls' safety every minute they were hiking through the woods.

4.   The lecture was supposed to be held at the seminar room but was moved to the auditorium to accommodate the crowd at the door.

5. The children were tired at the endless bickering of their parents.

6. Even though I was intensely jealous by his success, I made myself
   congratulate him being made a partner in the firm.

7. The detective was suspicious of every move the suspect made after eight
   o'clock the night of the robbery.

8. Will social security still be available to take care for our needs when we
   retire?

9. He was never sorry of any unkind words he said.

10. The students found it very hard to concentrate their studies after the fire
    alarm went off for the third time.

63–2 IDIOMATIC STRUCTURES

Edit the following sentences, making sure that idiomatic expressions with verbs and verbals are used correctly. If a sentence is correct, write "correct" after it. If you need help with this exercise, see Sections 63c–f in *Keys for Writers: A Brief Handbook*.

Example: **The owners and the players held talks for three days. They broke**

off them when they couldn't agree on any of the issues on the table.

a. My cousin told me to look up him if I was ever in Idaho.

b. Do you think she takes after her mother or her father?

c. The team members counted to the high-scoring forward to make up for their shaky defense.

d. Whenever she lists the seven capital sins, she leaves sloth.

e. The students were looking forward to travel to Washington during spring break.

1. The test was canceled because of the snowstorm, so we have to make up it next Saturday.

2. Before the surgeon general's warnings, many pregnant women used to drink alcohol without thinking about it.

3. Looking at the crowd lined at the front door, the soup kitchen volunteers were afraid they might run out bread.

4. If you're unsure of an answer, leave out it and go back if you have time at the end.

5. My younger sister always got away things I was punished for.

6. In the textile mills young girls worked for more than eight hours without to take a break.

7. When we moved to the Northeast we had to get used to shovel snow and scrape ice off our cars every morning.

8. The journalist ended up in jail because he stood up to what he thought was right.

9. What kinds of role models do young people look up today?

10. After three attacks in the campus parking lot, the university police decided to look in adding extra patrols.

65–1 GLOSSARY OF USAGE

Circle the word choice that correctly completes each sentence. If you need help with this exercise, see Section 65 in *Keys for Writers: A Brief Handbook.*

Example: **Athletes perform all kinds of bizarre and (incredible, incredulous) stunts in the world of so-called extreme sports.**

a. A new sport known as "extreme ironing" combines death-defying feats with an (everyday, every day) household chore.

b. Participants in the sport are known as "ironists," a name that may also (allude, elude) to their sense of humor.

c. The (cite, site, sight) of a person ironing on a mountain peak may become more common if extreme ironing gains popularity.

d. The sport seems comical, but only a committed participant would be willing to make a (decent, descent, dissent) from a mountain while carrying an ironing board.

e. Extreme ironing may have the (affect, effect) of making a dull task entertaining.

1. Philip Shaw, extreme ironing's creator, felt (disinterested, uninterested) in ironing his laundry at home one afternoon and ironed while rock climbing instead.

2. A Web (cite, site, sight) devoted to extreme ironing shows photographs of people ironing shirts on cliffs, in mid-air, and under water.

3. At the first extreme-ironing world championship in 2002, contestants (preceded, proceeded) through an obstacle course that required them to iron several garments.

4. Extreme ironing (maybe, may be) unlikely to appear in the Olympic Games in the near future, but a British team attracted a sponsor for the world championships.

5. Team members got (their, there, they're) irons from a French appliance company, which also paid for travel expenses and team shirts.

65–2 GLOSSARY OF USAGE

Correct any usage errors in the following passage. If you need help with this exercise, see Section 65 in *Keys for Writers: A Brief Handbook.*

Many Americans who want to keep saltwater fish as pets are concerned about the environmental affect of fishing on the coral reefs where tropical fish live. Because of saltwater fish are increasingly popular, these concerns are important. People who catch fish for the pet market often live in developing countries. These people can earn hundreds of dollars per pound selling pet fish, far more then they make catching fish to eat. Some fish collectors determined to catch the maximum number of fish use poisons, as cyanide, or explosives to stun fish. These kind of fishing techniques can kill off the coral (and frequently the fish), destroying the ecosystem that fishing communities rely on for food and income—a result that benefits nobody.

Marine biologists are hopeful, however, that the boom in saltwater fish sales may eventually result in less problems with coral reefs around the world. Pet owners can help by pressuring suppliers not to carry fish caught using elicit techniques. Many suppliers have been working for sometime to convince local fishers to use practices that protect the reef environment and the fish. The fishers, who's income depends on the coral being alive and well, recognize that they and they're families will suffer if a reef dies off. Therefore, they too work to protect the valuable fish and coral. The result benefits everyone—local people have wealthier communities, the oceans have healthier reefs, and aquariums have plenty of beautiful fish.

ANSWERS TO LETTERED EXERCISES

29–1 REPETITION AND REDUNDANCY, page 1

Suggested revisions:

a. Harold thought that if he submitted his resignation the group would fall apart.
b. Every candidate for the scholarship must provide two letters of reference.
c. From the airplane we could see coral reefs in the blue-green Caribbean.
d. We were hoping to find a motel with a decent restaurant and a laundry.
e. Parkinson's Law states that work expands to fill the time available for its completion.

30–1 ACTION VERBS, page 3

Suggested revisions:

a. Thirteen children have signed up to go to the Museum of Science.
b. She wrote a letter complaining about the poor service at the post office.
c. We preferred taking an early flight.
d. I have only one more thing to do before I leave for Seattle.
e. Maurice will not make it to the major leagues this year.

30–2 UNNECESSARY PASSIVE VOICE, page 4

a. My daughter's first-grade teacher has assigned too much homework.
b. Correct
c. Our neighbor fed the cats while we were out of town.
d. He had neatly arranged his father's old records on the shelf.
e. Correct

31–1   COORDINATION, SUBORDINATION, AND TRANSITIONS, page 6

Suggested revisions:

a. All students should learn how to use computers, for they will play an ever larger part in our future.
b. Marco hasn't turned in a single paper this semester; in fact, he hasn't turned in a piece of homework.
c. We could study at the park tomorrow if it doesn't rain, or we could study at the library if it does.
d. John F. Kennedy was president for less than three years, yet he was one of our most admired presidents.
e. Samantha's grades were better this semester than last; moreover, she was happier.

33–1   APPROPRIATE LANGUAGE, page 10

Suggested revisions:

a. I went to the car dealer to buy a new car.
b. Taking advantage of a chance to make a profit, the board of directors voted to sell the radio station.
c. My boss rejected my idea, saying it was not workable.
d. While staying in Beverly Hills, they took a walk in the neighborhood where movie stars live.
e. Lack of rainfall and very high temperatures threaten the corn crop.

33–2   APPROPRIATE LANGUAGE, page 11

Suggested revisions:

a. With tires screaming, the police car sped off after the robbers.
b. The supervisor met with each department head before the sales conference.
c. The novel is definitely a masterpiece.
d. I asked my parents for the car, but my sister had already asked them.
e. Our captain tried to motivate us for the big game.

33–3 APPROPRIATE LANGUAGE, page 12

Suggested revisions:

a. Each supervisor was warned that the workers might strike without notice.
b. All the congressional representatives on the committee voted to send the bill to the full House.
c. The new clinic helps patients with breast cancer.
d. The Girl Scouts staffed the table in front of the grocery store to sell cookies.
e. Off-duty police officers sometimes encounter crimes in progress.

34–1 SENTENCE TYPES, page 13

a. Compound
b. Complex; dependent clauses: Whereas an ophthalmologist is a medical doctor, who specializes in the eyes
c. Compound-complex; dependent clause: Unless you tell us otherwise
d. Simple
e. Compound

37–2 PARTS OF SPEECH: NOUNS, page 16

a. election, chairperson, commission, times
b. Ben Franklin, name, Poor Richard, almanac
c. chickens, pen
d. building's, owner, buyers
e. Ticks, time, skin

37–3 PARTS OF SPEECH: PRONOUNS, page 17

Suggested answers:

a. who, she
b. Everyone
c. My, I, them
d. This, mine, yours
e. himself, his

37–4 PARTS OF SPEECH: VERBS, page 18

a. V: praised
b. V: know; LV: is; AUX: Do
c. LV: is, is
d. V: ran
e. V: know, disappeared, telling; AUX: am

37–5 PARTS OF SPEECH: ADJECTIVES, page 19

Suggested answers:

a. The had to prepare two bedrooms because their sprightly aunt and elderly grandmother were coming to visit.
b. My stubborn dog has been very disobedient since I took her to obedience school.
c. Our paper was supposed to be on a Dickens novel.
d. After a late night of partying, we were not very energetic at the next morning's classes.
e. They had to wade through shallow water to reach the dilapidated boat tied to the white dock.

37–6 PARTS OF SPEECH: ADVERBS, page 21

Suggested answers:

a. I had to hire someone to organize my files efficiently.
b. The painting was a quite remarkable achievement.
c. The swallows return faithfully to Capistrano every March.
d. He was running out of time, so he had to write hastily in his blue book.
e. The concert attracted nearly one hundred thousand people on a somewhat chilly June night.

37–7 PARTS OF SPEECH: PREPOSITIONS, page 22

Suggested answers:

a. The sailors returned home weary after the voyage.
b. We looked over the edge at the green valley below.
c. I've never known true peace until now.

d. Through the long night the father sat by his baby's side.

e. Between the bridges flowed a teeming river.

37–8 PARTS OF SPEECH: CONJUNCTIONS, page 23

Suggested answers:

a. Vera had looked forward to reading the new novel, so she was disappointed that it was so boring. (coordinating conjunction)

b. Lukas crept quietly toward the deer and the fawn because he wanted to take pictures of them. (subordinating conjunction)

c. She tried to sleep whenever the sound of sirens diminished. (subordinating conjunction)

d. We can't bring any food to camp; moreover, we will receive mail only twice a week. (conjunctive adverb)

e. As visitors lined up outside the museum entrance, officials tried to decide whether to open the doors early. (subordinating conjunction)

38–1 SENTENCE FRAGMENTS, page 25

Suggested revisions:

a. I'll be happy to help you if I have the time.

b. Since 1979, because of a proposal made by the United States, the World Meteorological Organization has given hurricanes male and female names.

c. Correct

d. Captain Lowry was irritated by the poem honoring veterans of the armed forces when she realized that the poet seemed to think that only men had served in the military.

e. In my culture, which feels that women are not as important as men, it is a constant struggle for a woman to gain the respect of a man.

38–2 SENTENCE FRAGMENTS, page 27

Suggested revisions:

a. My husband and I are always running out of money by the end of the month.
b. Knowing that Jakob would be there, I hurried home to see my long-lost cousin.
c. The Vietnam Memorial, near the Lincoln Memorial, was dedicated on November 13, 1982.
d. My brother couldn't decide whether to name his first baby Edison or Harrison—after the inventor or the actor.
e. The lawn needs fertilizer and seed in the spring, and it needs mowing and watering in the summer.

39–1 RUN-ONS AND COMMA SPLICES, page 30

Suggested revisions:

a. Some people love celebrating their birthdays, but some people would just as soon forget them.
b. I know someone who maxed out four credit cards, so she paid them off and cut them up.
c. My mother always said, "Don't run down the stairs." She was right.
d. When we were children, our parents let us sell lemonade in front of our house; times have changed, however.
e. He's not working now; he's still at home.

39–2 RUN-ONS AND COMMA SPLICES, page 32

Suggested revisions:

a. At the only supermarket in town, apples from New Zealand cost less than locally grown apples. That doesn't make sense.
b. Correct
c. Petra dedicated her life to Paul; in return he dedicated his life to his job.
d. Last month our middle school sponsored a "TV turnoff," the purpose of which was to show children that they can have fun without watching television.
e. You need to plan now; otherwise your retirement income will be too little for you to live on.

40–1 SENTENCE SNARLS: DANGLING AND MISPLACED MODIFIERS, page 34

Suggested revisions:

a. She asked whether the butcher shop that we frequently patronize has fresh turkey.

b. Visitors can journey back to a town that, nestled between two mountains, has remained unchanged for two centuries.

c. By the day after Christmas, the children had broken almost all their toys.

d. Sensing that the students weren't prepared, Mr. Sanchez postponed the pop quiz.

e. Having finished nearly all the pie, we wrapped the rest in plastic wrap.

40–2 SENTENCE SNARLS: DANGLING AND MISPLACED MODIFIERS, page 36

Suggested revisions:

a. The archaeologists found almost an entire dinosaur skeleton.

b. Because the automobile insurance cost more than we expected, we could afford only the legal minimum amount.

c. The job that she thought would completely hold her interest bored her. *Or* The job that she thought would hold her interest bored her completely.

d. Eager to see Fort Sumter, we took the tour boat across Charleston Harbor.

e. The picnic table and benches that we just finished painting are on the lawn.

40–3 SENTENCE SNARLS: SHIFTS, MIXED CONSTRUCTIONS, DEFINITIONS, AND REASONS, page 38

Suggested revisions:

a. Cattle contract mad cow disease when they eat meat that contains infectious proteins that cause normal proteins in the brain to unfold.

b. Our professor told us to pick up our blue books before we sat down but not to start writing until she gave us final instructions.

c. The reason the heat came on is that the temperature outside dropped below fifty degrees. *Or* The heat came on because the temperature outside dropped below fifty degrees.

d. The IRS agent demanded that Maureen bring all her receipts for the past year as well as her daily calendar and her checkbook.

e. To do a handspring full twist, the gymnast pushes off the floor with both hands, snaps her feet around over her head, pushes off with her feet, and does a 360-degree twist in the air before landing.

40–4 SENTENCE SNARLS: SUBJECT-PREDICATE MISMATCH, page 40

Suggested revisions:

a. Climbing the last thousand feet of the Mauna Kea volcano made us dizzy and lightheaded.
b. As an African American student who went to a high school in Brooklyn that had a student body seventy percent white, I sometimes could not face one more day in school.
c. Abraham's attempt to appear polite and gracious backfired and made him appear rude and ungrateful.
d. Her weightlifting over the winter has improved Mary Jane's effectiveness as a power pitcher.
e. For all your absences this semester, your grade will drop by half a point.

40–5 SENTENCE SNARLS: ADVERB CLAUSE AS SUBJECT, OMITTED WORDS, AND RESTATED SUBJECT, page 42

Suggested revisions:

a. Noriaki's depression contributes to his family's concern.
b. My aunt and uncle can live and have lived for years without leaving the island.
c. All the neighbors wondered how the two boys could possibly get away with such a blatant crime.
d. The hothouse tomatoes from the farm stand are as expensive as but tastier than those from the gourmet market.
e. The child who wandered into the aisle during the service was quickly snatched up by her mother.

40–6 SENTENCE SNARLS: FAULTY PARALLELISM, page 44

Suggested revisions:

a. To be comfortable at the campsite, they not only wanted to light a decent fire for cooking but also needed to have access to an electrical hookup.
b. Tom liked bowling on Saturday afternoons and fishing with his neighbor.
c. Listening to the crickets chirp in the country is better than being bombarded by traffic noise in the city.
d. Bella could throw a boomerang with accuracy, clean a trout in under a minute, and paddle a canoe expertly.
e. Betsy was overjoyed and excited when she heard the news.

41–1 REGULAR AND IRREGULAR VERB FORMS, AUXILIARIES, AND MODALS, page 46

Suggested revisions:

a. We had driven fifteen miles before Mark told us about the money he had lost gambling last week.
b. Correct
c. She had gone with him five times before her parents found out.
d. She set the keys on the table with such a crash that it woke the cat.
e. I might not win the contest, but I have made a good attempt.

41–2 VERB TENSES, page 48

Suggested revisions:

a. ran
b. will be doing
c. is
d. embodies
e. had worked, postponed

41–3 VERB TENSES, page 50

Suggested revisions:

a. They will not take a vote until all the committee members are seated.
b. Some people look away when they see an accident, but I like to study such things.
c. They owned the business for twenty-five years.
d. Battles used to be fought with battering rams and siege engines, which were used to penetrate castle defenses.
e. The football coach got so upset by the call that he stuck his head in the water bucket.

41–4 VERBS: *-ED* ENDINGS, page 52

Suggested revisions:

a. Our office changed to a new computer system last month, and most of us still haven't figured it out.
b. Because she had had four years of Italian in high school, she was able to skip to the advanced course in freshman year of college.
c. After eight hours, he had accomplished his goal of sanding the entire face of the house.
d. The school committee decided to postpone a vote on the proposed renovations to the middle school.
e. Once the conversation turned to adult matters, Celia excused herself from the table and went to her room.

41–5 VERBS IN CONDITIONAL SENTENCES AND IN WISHES, REQUESTS, AND DEMANDS, page 54

Suggested revisions:

a. When the temperature drops below thirty-two degrees, water freezes.
b. If the workers voted today, they would not be able to agree on a settlement with management.
c. She would have known that the butler was innocent if she had kept careful notes and had paid attention to the witnesses.
d. If he were sixty-two, he would retire without a second thought.
e. The principal demanded that we bring a note from our parents about our absence.

41–6 VERB FORMS AND TENSES, page 56

a. Does a person need to be thin and muscular to be attractive?

b. Weight gain, triggered by changing body chemistry, is common when girls reach puberty.

c. Although people are increasingly aware of the damage dieting can do to young bodies, the number of teenagers and pre-teens obsessed with becoming thinner continues to rise.

d. Correct

e. If young people were more aware of the artifice required to produce the seemingly perfect people in music videos and fashion magazines, teenagers might not have such unrealistic expectations of how they should look.

42–1 PASSIVE VOICE, page 58

Suggested revisions:

a. After the bombs had been dropped, a spy plane assessed the damage.

b. The blood samples are being analyzed for their DNA content.

c. Correct

d. The audience at the magic show was stumped when a girl in the audience was turned into a crow.

e. Two dozen witnesses were questioned in the case.

43–1 SUBJECT-VERB AGREEMENT, page 60

a. knows

b. leads

c. talk

d. are

e. has

43–2 SUBJECT-VERB AGREEMENT, page 62

a. There were an otter and three whales at Point Lobos yesterday.

b. Her grades are the only thing that matters to her parents.

c. The home unit of the soldiers who were lost last week is throwing them a party.

d. At the start of the movie, from the depths of the seas emerges a magnificent whale.

e. Do the butter and the sugar go into the bowl before the flour?

43–3 SUBJECT-VERB AGREEMENT, page 64

a. Correct
b. Recycling or bringing trash to local dumps is recommended for trash removal.
c. Either the sculpture or the paintings are intended for the foyer.
d. For several seconds after the curtain came down, there was neither clapping nor cheering.
e. Several cookies in the last batch were burned.

43–4 SUBJECT-VERB AGREEMENT, page 65

a. Correct
b. Either of her teachers was willing to give her credit for effort.
c. A great deal of pain and suffering was a natural by-product of the explosion.
d. The dance troupe wasn't ready to perform, and it showed.
e. The wrappings from a hasty lunch were left on the desk.

44–1 PRONOUN FORMS, page 66

a. Is it okay for you and me to go to the play today?
b. Our lockers are clean; theirs are a mess.
c. Albert thinks that no one can jump better than he.
d. Correct
e. He didn't like my singing along with the record.

44–2 PRONOUN REFERENCE, page 68

Suggested revisions:

a. I got a letter from the bank about a bounced check, but no one answered the phone when I called to explain.
b. In his work, Tim O'Brien recounts in many different forms his experiences in Vietnam.
c. After an adventurous first lesson, José told Bruce that Bruce would never learn to drive. *Or* After an adventurous first lesson, José told Bruce, "I will never learn to drive."
d. The newspaper article says that children today spend more time watching TV than their parents did.

e. I planted a bush in the garden next to the house; now I just have to remember to water the garden every day. *Or* I planted a bush in the garden next to the house; now I just have to remember to water the bush every day.

44–3 PRONOUN AGREEMENT, page 70

Suggested revisions:

a. All students must know their Social Security numbers.
b. In its year-end report, the company gave its stockholders the bad news.
c. Every job applicant is required to state whether he or she has been convicted of any crimes in the past five years. *Or* All job applicants are required to state whether they have been convicted of any crimes in the past five years.
d. Everyone on the boys' soccer team is responsible for keeping his own uniform clean.
e. Correct

44–4 FORMS OF THE PRONOUNS *WHO* AND *WHOEVER,* page 72

a. Give this book to whoever wants it.
b. I asked the manager who was in charge of customer service.
c. Correct
d. Whom should we ask to play the piano, her or Lupè?
e. She wrote an article about whom the coach intended to use in the next game.

45–1 ADJECTIVES AND ADVERBS, page 73

a. If you don't do well on the test, you may have to repeat the course.
b. He acted so unreasonably that we had to leave the party early.
c. She darted quickly between the opposing players and then dribbled swiftly for the basket.
d. They could scarcely contain their excitement on arriving in Rome.
e. The moon did not appear very bright even though it was full tonight.

45–2 PLACEMENT OF ADVERBS, page 75

Possible revisions:

a. I pulled the emergency brake immediately.
b. The buttons were sewn perfectly onto the sweater.
c. The telephone always rang when he was trying to sleep.
d. The rain fell steadily throughout the day.
e. Never will I go back to that store.

45–3 COMPARATIVE AND SUPERLATIVE FORMS OF ADJECTIVES AND ADVERBS, page 76

Suggested revisions:

a. He claimed that his expensive new shoes helped him to run more quickly than he'd ever run before.
b. The larger of my feet is a full half-inch longer than the smaller.
c. Henry's painting is good, but Carmen's is even better.
d. No one could feel worse than I feel today.
e. My sister and I were always competitive, but we reached a silent agreement: she was more artistic but I was smarter.

45–4 FAULTY OR INCOMPLETE COMPARISONS, page 78

Suggested revisions:

a. Joanna's pet fish has more fins than her boyfriend's.
b. Forest walks his own dog more often than his son's.
c. Celia wants a vacation more than her fiancé does.
d. Correct
e. The review said the famous director's new movie was less self-indulgent than his last one.

46–1 RELATIVE CLAUSES AND RELATIVE PRONOUNS, page 79

a. We ordered trophies for all the players who we feel deserve recognition.
b. We always prefer to debate with people who express opinions forcefully.
c. Runners who stretch before they run have fewer injuries than those who don't stretch.

d. Correct

e. One of the violinists who play in the pops orchestra will be selected to join the symphony orchestra at the end of the season.

46–2 RELATIVE CLAUSES AND RELATIVE PRONOUNS, page 80

a. My mother, who has worked all her life, will finally retire in July.

b. The paper that we were assigned on October 10 is due on November 10.

c. The word *awesome,* which I use all the time, does not really mean "interesting" or "cool."

d. The counselor to whom I referred my brother was kind enough to find time in her schedule for him.

e. Students who study every day fare better on tests than students who cram the night before.

47–1 COMMAS: COORDINATION AND INTRODUCTORY ELEMENTS, page 82

a. Unlike the national security adviser, the senator believed that the president needed a full accounting of events.

b. She does not know who her secret admirer is, but she appreciates the attention.

c. Wearing a beaded collar, the poodle pranced around the ring.

d. After mowing and trimming, the lawn looked like a velvet carpet.

e. Correct

47–2 COMMAS: NONRESTRICTIVE ELEMENTS AND TRANSITIONAL EXPRESSIONS, page 84

a. Alaska, the forty-ninth state, and Hawaii, the fiftieth, were both admitted to the Union in 1959.

b. We continue to assert, however, that dogs abandoned by their owners should first be offered to the public for adoption.

c. John Wesley Powell, who led geological expeditions into Colorado and Utah, had lost an arm during the Civil War.

d. Nevertheless, he decided to brave the storm and drive home.

e. Correct

47–3 COMMAS: MISCELLANEOUS USES, page 85

a. It was a hot, smoggy, and depressing day.
b. I opened the door, looked around the room, and finally spotted the raincoat I'd forgotten.
c. December 7, 1941, was the date that President Roosevelt said would "live in infamy."
d. Correct
e. Joan Bergmann, L.L.D., opened her solo office as soon as she graduated from law school.

47–4 COMMAS: MISUSES, page 87

a. We should not necessarily think that he is the one to blame.
b. Eleven very tired Brownies and their adult leaders were happy to go home after the overnight camping trip.
c. Correct
d. Dixie, Peanuts, and Clement were what we called the puppies.
e. There are too many tomatoes in the soup and not enough carrots.

48–1 APOSTROPHES, page 89

a. I'll sew the costumes if you'll paint the sets.
b. Sarah liked to look at her brothers' record album covers from the '60s.
c. My sister-in-law's house is more than 150 years old; its most interesting feature is a hidden passageway in the library.
d. When we visited Ireland, we tried to locate the Murphys, who used to live next door to us.
e. Their house is on the sunny side of the street; ours is on the shady side.

49–1 QUOTATION MARKS, page 90

a. Why were we assigned Doris Lessing's story "The Old Chief Mshlanga"?
b. The judge asked whether the jury had reached a verdict.
c. Our parents used to think that lyrics like "I want to hold your hand" were profound.
d. "I think that I shall never see / A billboard lovely as a tree," Ogden Nash wrote, in parody of Joyce Kilmer's poem "Trees."
e. The teacher asked, "Who said, 'Give me liberty or give me death'?"

49–2 QUOTATION MARKS, page 92

a. A song-and-dance sequence is considered essential for a mainstream Bollywood film.
b. The 2002 film *Bhoot,* which means "ghost," surprised audiences by becoming a hit in spite of its lack of songs.
c. Shailaja Neelakanten's online article about a renegade Bollywood director, Ram Gopal Varma, was called "Bollywood's Tarantino and His Band of Outsiders."
d. "The Art of Advertising," a chapter of *Cinema India* by Rachel Dwyer and Divia Patel, takes an in-depth look at movie posters.
e. Popular Bollywood hits have been based on characters from Hindu mythology and on Shakespeare's *Romeo and Juliet* and other plays.

50–1 SEMICOLONS, page 94

Suggested revisions:

a. Mary has lived in many places: Newark, New Jersey; Charleston, South Carolina; Miami, Florida; and Austin, Texas.
b. It snowed very little that winter; nevertheless, sales of ski equipment soared.
c. True friends exhibit four main qualities: openness, trust, loyalty, and love.
d. The county's water shortage was severe. Many restaurants in the area stopped serving water with meals unless a customer specifically requested it.
e. Correct

50–2 COLONS, page 96

Suggested revisions:

a. His plan was obvious: break the window, cut the wires, snatch the jewels, and sneak down the fire escape.
b. My favorite Gospel story is that of the Samaritan woman at the well in John 4:9–30.
c. For her driving test, Monica hoped for a kind inspector, no yellow lights, no oncoming traffic, and no empty parking spots for parallel parking.
d. Brendel was ready to go to his job interview, but there was one small problem: he couldn't find his car keys.
e. Correct

51–1 PERIODS, QUESTION MARKS, AND EXCLAMATION POINTS, page 98

a. Would you please give me a call as soon as you're ready?

b. "Are you crazy?" he asked.

c. "The tornado is heading straight for us!" he screamed. "Run for your life!"

d. My younger sister spent a week at a space camp run by NASA.

e. With parents like that, is it any wonder that he's always late?

51–2 DASHES, PARENTHESES, BRACKETS, SLASHES, AND ELLIPSIS DOTS, page 99

Suggested revisions:

a. Shirley St. Hill Chisholm (who was the country's first African American Congresswoman) used the campaign slogan "Unbought and Unbossed."

b. The judge said, "You [the defendant] are a menace to society."

c. His final shot—what a blast!—sank through the basket just as the buzzer sounded.

d. The monetary part of the award ($50) wasn't nearly as important as the recognition.

e. In her last speech to Torvald, Nora declares her independence: "I'm freeing you from being responsible. . . . There has to be absolute freedom for us both" (64).

52–1 UNDERLINING (ITALICS), page 101

a. The French use the term *bon appetit* at the beginning of a meal; many Americans now say simply, "Enjoy."

b. The poem "Video Cuisine" appears in Maxine Kumin's collection *The Long Approach.*

c. My two-year-old uses the word *dog* to refer to any animal.

d. Most Americans know the Latin word for *tree,* which is *arbor.*

e. I've seen the movie *Master and Commander* four times, and I intend to see it at least four more.

53–1 CAPITALIZATION, page 102

a. Correct
b. The Republican Party was known as the antislavery party at the time of the Civil War.
c. During fall semester our architecture class visited Rockefeller Center, the Empire State Building, and St. Patrick's Cathedral.
d. Mahatma Gandhi applied the principles of civil disobedience to his struggle for Indian independence.
e. Virginia Cusack, executive vice president, was known to most of the workers as Ginny.

54–1 ABBREVIATIONS, page 103

a. Dr. Roya Mullen was my pediatrician, and now she is my children's.
b. The students wondered how they would get through all of chapter 5 in one night.
c. Correct
d. The men voted to stay overnight in New York City, but the women voted to continue on to Philadelphia.
e. The FBI, the CIA, and the IRS don't have the best reputations with the American public.

55–1 NUMBERS, page 104

a. On December 7, 1941, Japanese planes attacked Pearl Harbor.
b. Correct
c. To get ready for the race, Yvonne ran three miles one day, five miles the next, and eight miles the next.
d. Nell took exactly $9.25 from her piggy bank when she went to the arcade.
e. Twelve times this year I've asked my neighbors to keep their dog tied up during the day when they're at work.

56–1 HYPHENATION, page 105

a. After the accident, Jake was semiconscious, and it took him forty-five minutes to remember his own name.
b. Three-quarters of the way through the test, I realized I didn't remember enough about post-Reconstruction America to answer the last essay question.
c. The short-term profit was a relief to the fledgling CEO.

d. Her way-out ideas have led to some really innovative advances in medical treatment.

e. The half-price items at the hardware store included a gas-powered leaf blower.

58–1 SPELLING, page 106

a. Gertrude was very embarrassed when her pocketbook spilled open on the subway train.

b. Most young people want independence from their parents, but many of them also want their parents to continue to support them, if only emotionally.

c. Correct

d. My sociology professor is very knowledgeable, but sometimes her knowledge interferes with common sense.

e. Our seventh-grade teacher always told us that our grammar was good but that we misspelled too much.

58–2 SPELLING, page 108

a. leaves

b. perceive

c. offered

d. Correct

e. prettiest

60–1 CATEGORIES OF NOUNS AND NOUN PLURALS, page 109

a. The Volga River (P) is the longest river (CC) in Europe (P).

b. Many people (CC) believe they have been abducted by aliens (CC) from space (UC).

c. Times Square (P) has experienced a renaissance (CC) in recent years (CC).

d. The *New York Times* (P) employs many excellent reporters (CC).

e. Jell-O (P) is a brand (CC) of gelatin (UC) frequently used in making low-fat desserts (CC).

60–2 NOUNS AND ARTICLES, page 110

a. The line of tourists at the White House was already quite long, winding along the street next to the White House lawn toward a park called the Ellipse.
b. I walked around the Ellipse and up a small hill to the Washington Monument.
c. The line there was not as long, so I waited underneath the circle of fifty flags, one for every state in the United States.
d. From information in my guidebook, I learned that the monument is 555 feet tall and was the tallest structure in the world when it was built in 1886.
e. From the observation area at the top of the monument I could see all of Washington spread out before me.

60–3 NOUNS AND ARTICLES, page 112

Suggested revisions:

a. I put a potato in the oven and then went out to the store. An hour later I had to phone my sister and ask her to take the potato out of the oven.
b. Money can't buy happiness, but it can pay the grocery bill.
c. Which country in South America is your roommate from?
d. Jorge asked his mother for advice about living away from home for the first time.
e. She ordered a hamburger and fries. The fries were delivered first; by the time the hamburger arrived at her table, she had finished eating all the fries.

61–1 THE *BE* AUXILIARY, page 114

Suggested revisions:

a. They are eating now.
b. The pool was drained last month.
c. The skyscraper was built in only three months.
d. Correct
e. Ivan has been taking an art class for six weeks.

61–2 MODAL AUXILIARY VERBS, page 115

Suggested answers:

a. should sleep
b. must have locked
c. would have set
d. must wash
e. could, get

61–3 VERBS FOLLOWED BY AN INFINITIVE OR *-ING* VERBAL, page 117

a. The pilot ordered the passengers to turn off their cell phones for the rest of the flight.
b. The committee discussed adopting the proposal but postponed voting on it until the next meeting.
c. On her first trip to Hawaii, she could not imagine being in a more beautiful place on Earth.
d. Tony persuaded his mother to allow him to take the family car overnight.
e. We can no longer pretend to be uninvolved.

61–4 VERBALS USED AS ADJECTIVES, page 119

a. I am always annoyed by my little brother's early morning noise when I am trying to sleep late.
b. The statistics on underage drinking and driving are very depressing.
c. Sarah reluctantly brought her disappointing first-semester report card home to her parents.
d. The worried director made her exhausted cast run through the play one more time.
e. We couldn't imagine a more boring lecture, but we kept ourselves amused by passing notes across the back row.

62–1 SENTENCE STRUCTURE, page 120

Suggested revisions:

a. The committee sent a subpoena to the alleged witness.
b. Professor Moran explained exponential functions to the class.

   c. Correct

   d. The meteorology students visited Mount Washington yesterday.

   e. Bob ran every morning because it helped him keep in shape.

62–2 DIRECT AND INDIRECT QUOTATIONS AND QUESTIONS, page 121

Suggested revisions:

   a. During the inquiry, he kept repeating that he didn't see a thing.

   b. The woman at the garden shop told us to plant the impatiens in a shady corner of the flowerbed.

   c. She asked if I wanted to taste the brownies. I said that sure, I wanted to taste them.

   d. My cousin asked if I remembered the summer we spent on Granddad's farm.

   e. As she stepped out of the car at the airport terminal, Carla told her father not to bother, that she could handle her bags herself.

62–3 ORDER OF ADJECTIVES, page 122

   a. She became a genuine American celebrity.

   b.   He plans the giant annual Greek Orthodox Easter picnic in the park.

   c. To cheer me up on this dreary day, I brought along my huge new flowered umbrella.

   d.   A small yellow shed stands at the end of her new wooden walkway in the garden.

   e. The panting, yapping dog dashed madly around our ankles, hoping for a walk.

63–1 IDIOMATIC STRUCTURES, page 124

   a. In May, the dissatisfied passenger wrote a letter complaining about the lack of food on the four-hour train trip.

   b. She has always been interested in features on the moon.

   c. When we arrived in Florence, we weren't sure whether to go to the Duomo or the Uffizi first.

   d. He was content with his low-paying entry-level job because it left him time for his real passion: scuba diving.

   e. She was very anxious about losing the ticket until her uncle found it lying on the couch.

63–2 IDIOMATIC STRUCTURES, page 126

Suggested revisions:

a. My cousin told me to look him up if I was ever in Idaho.
b. Correct
c. The team members counted on the high-scoring forward to make up for their shaky defense.
d. Whenever she lists the seven capital sins, she leaves out sloth.
e. The students were looking forward to traveling to Washington during spring break.

65–1 GLOSSARY OF USAGE, page 128

a. everyday
b. allude
c. sight
d. descent
e. effect